The Golden Years
Healthy Aging & the Older Adult

Christopher W. Bogosh

Good Samaritan Books
Keeping hope and comfort in Jesus Christ
www.goodsamaritanbooks.org

The Golden Years: Healthy Aging & the Older Adult
Copyright © 2013 Christopher W. Bogosh
Published by Good Samaritan Books
   86395 Riverwood Drive
   Yulee, FL 32097
   www.goodsamaritanbooks.org

Printed in the United States of America.

Unless otherwise indicated, Bible quotations are taken from *New International Version* of the Bible. Copyright © 1973, 1978, 1984 by the International Bible Society. All rights reserved.

ISBN: 1481077740
ISBN-13: 978-1481077743

The silver-haired head is a crown of glory, if it is found in the way of righteousness.
(Pro. 16:31, NKJ)

CONTENTS

PREFACE

I once heard someone say, "old age is not all it is cut out to be," and although I am not ready to sit in a rocking chair, I am certainly old enough to know what it means to be an older adult. A couple of years ago, I enrolled in Medicare; my body feels the sixty-five plus years of my existence. My wife and I have our share of aches, pains, and chronic ailments. I have also been involved in the care of my aged father, suffering a stroke at eighty-eight, and living a bedbound existence until his death at ninety. Presently, I am caring for my ninety-three old mother struggling with advanced heart disease, who is contemplating her mortality on a daily basis. Not to mention my service as a pastor for the last thirty years, this has exposed me to the unique difficulties older adults and adult children face. I am keenly, and even painfully, aware of the need to live out "the golden years" with physical, mental, and spiritual fitness.

Chris has done a great service in writing *The Golden Years* to help people do this. Not only for the church, but also for people everywhere facing the issues older adults, adult children, and people caring for the elderly face. Chris is well qualified to write on this subject. He is a registered nurse, serving the older adult population in the field of hospice care. Chris is also theologically educated, possessing a deep appreciation for the authority of Scripture. He writes with a unique blend of biblical love and medical expertise. I give thanks for his teaching, preaching, and counsel at New Hope Baptist Church. I am grateful to be his pastor.

In this volume, Chris reminds the reader about often forgotten commonsense approaches to healthcare. There is valuable instruction about good health practices, especially in the areas of nutrition and exercise. Some of the most helpful counsel focuses on navigating the confusing world of professional health care and medical science from a biblical perspective. Chris does an excellent job addressing highly technical and complex matters in an understandable manner. Most importantly, readers will cultivate a God-honoring view on how to live out "the golden years" in a biblical context.

Even if you are not ready to join the "senior circuit," this book is important to read. One day all of us will have family members or friends advancing in years in need of help and wise counsel. With life expectancy in America approaching ninety and new changes to Medicare, it makes good sense to be prepared and use healthcare wisely. The information gained from this book will prove valuable, both now, and for years to come. After reading *The Golden Years*, I suspect you will want to purchase copies for others, so that they too will gain a valuable perspective on the, "way that they have not passed before" (Josh. 3:4, KJV).

Pastor George Anderson
New Hope Baptist Church
Saint Marys, Georgia

1

THE OLDER
ADULT

"**M**y serve," I said, trying to catch my breath, "three to fourteen, ready?" Th-warp, bounce, bounce, squeak, th-warp, bounce, bounce, swish—"Ah, I missed! Your point. You win."

"Good game, ready to go again?"

"No, not today. I have a lot to do. Besides I'm exhausted! I need to hit the showers. I will look forward to seeing you tonight for our study in the Psalms."

"Great, Chris. Looking forward to it."

John beat me nearly every time we played racquetball. He was excellent at this high-intensity game, even at the ripe age of seventy-six! John was the epitome of good health.

When John was not beating me at racquetball, he took time to mentor me in the Christian faith. John was a godly man with knowledge, wisdom, insight, zeal, and an insatiable hunger for the Psalms.

John served in the Pacific theatre during World War II in the Philippines. During his tour, the Lord burdened John's heart for the Filipino people. After his discharge from the Army, he went to seminary, and he returned to the Philippines as a missionary. He served in the foreign mission field several years, and after John returned stateside, he served a church as its pastor. John cut down on his full-time ministerial duties after fifty years, but that did not stop his work for God. In fact, John and I met while he was serving as an interim pastor at the church I was a member.

At the time we met, I was in seminary. I knew about John's pastoral experience and extensive work in the Psalms, so I approached him and asked if he would be willing to serve as one of my mentors and teach me more about the Psalms. He agreed, provided I play racquetball. Therefore, from that point on, his mission in life was to bless me with his knowledge about the Psalms, and beat me at racquetball.

John was not disillusioned about his age either, hoping to feel younger by befriending a person less than half his age. He was well aware of the aches, pains, sorrows, and chronic health problems associated with aging. In fact, John's wife was sick with terminal cancer when I met him. John had a sober view of his mortality, but he also knew that with each breath he took, he drew closer to the time he would go to be with the God he loved and enjoyed.

Most importantly, John recognized his need to grow spiritually and stay healthy, even in this autumn stage of life. John's older adult years were not idle, nor were they fixated on him. Rather they were focused on others and serving them. John saw himself as an older adult possessing years of theological acumen, pastoral experience, wisdom, and unique spiritual gifts that God expected him to use and pass on to others. He also saw his body as a sacred gift given to him by God, so he took care of it by exercising, eating a proper diet, and by practicing preventive healthcare to age to the glory of God.

Facts about Aging and Health

According to the Administration on Aging, John lives among forty million Americans sixty-five and over. This accounts for 13 percent of the present population in the United States. In 2030, estimations predict that 20 percent of the American population will be over sixty-five. Life expectancy for people over sixty-five in the United States is eighty-two for males and eighty-five for females. There are about 70,000 people over one hundred in the United States, and projected calculations indicate that this will grow to an astonishing 381,000 by 2030. John is part of a rapidly growing subculture in the United

States, requiring a high level of commitment and competency for good health behaviors to occur.

Three major issues hinder older adults from practicing good health behaviors today: health literacy, financial resources, and lack of motivation. A program called Healthy People 2010 defined health literacy as, "The degree to which individuals have the capacity to obtain, process, and understand basic health information and services needed to make appropriate health decisions." This includes the ability to understand basic medical information, a healthcare provider's instructions, medical education brochures, informed consent documents, prescriptions, and over-the-counter medication labels. Older adults are at an increased risk for not comprehending this information and this contributes to poor health practices.

Another factor leading to poor health behavior is a lack of money. My wheezing mother recently shared with me that she was unable to buy her respiratory medication because it was too expensive. This is a bigger problem than recognized today, but it is a reality for older adults on fixed incomes. In fact, the addition of one medication may force an older adult to choose between the drug and eating breakfast in the morning. Health literacy and lack of finances are two obstacles to adequate health behaviors but the major barrier is motivation.

Lack of motivation is the major factor among older adults leading to poor health. My mentor and friend John was motivated to stay healthy as an older adult; unfortunately, according to the Center for Disease Control (CDC) this is not the norm. Reports from the CDC indicate that older adults do not regularly exercise, are overweight, and they do not eat enough fruits and vegetables. The CDC investigation found the major culprit to be lack of motivation, not inability, or access.

A study in the state of New Jersey indicated that 70 percent of the physical decline in older adults was due to poor health behaviors. Chronic disease conditions are not necessarily "in the genes," or a normal part of the aging process, according to the findings of this study. The study also found that good health behaviors actually prevent chronic conditions associated with aging, such as heart disease, arthritis, strokes, some types of cancer, and diabetes. The same study indicated that older adults with good health habits reduced their chance for chronic health conditions by 50 percent.

Good health behaviors and healthy aging provide more than physical wellbeing and longevity, they reduce chronic health conditions, and they enhance the older adult's life tremendously. As a result, older adults have the ability to remain independent longer, and most importantly, they will be able to serve others by blessing them with a life's worth of experience, wisdom, and insight.

According to a survey conducted by the Administration on Aging, healthy aging and good health behaviors equaled successful aging, defined by most older adults as possessing financial security, having basic needs met (food, clothing, companionship, etc.), feeling useful, and possessing the ability to engage in meaningful activities. In my opinion, my mentor and friend John was living healthy and aging successfully, and I am writing this book to help others do the same.

The Journey Ahead

I am dedicating *The Golden Years: Healthy Aging and the Older Adult* to older adults, adult children, family members, and caregivers—anyone involved with people over sixty-five. My purpose is to help the public gain a better understanding of aging, good health practices, preventive medicine, common problems associated with aging, and chronic conditions experienced by older adults. The chapters to follow will address each of these topics and more, including recent changes to Medicare by the Affordable Care Act (ACA).

In addition, the perceptive reader would have noticed already my Christian convictions. I am a Christian nurse with a pastoral education. Therefore, my writing is rooted in who I am, so the nursing-pastoral worldview presented in this book is biblically oriented. I believe with all my heart that "Jesus Christ is the same yesterday and today and forever" (Heb. 13:8), and, therefore, the Bible has relevance, guidance, and answers for us today.

I am indebted to the dedication, research, and expertise of Suzanne Fitzsimmons, MSN, ARNP, published in Western School's *Healthy Aging* and *Nursing Care of the Older Adult*. Rather than clutter this book with numerous citations from these two books, I will acknowledge her work now. All of the quantitative nursing and medical data, unless otherwise noted, is based upon her expertise and research in the field of geriatric medicine. In addition, all of the information provided in this book is just that—information. My suggestions do not replace the older adult's need for a healthcare provider. In fact, this book assumes interaction with a primary care provider for adequate healthcare.

Finally, also by way of disclosure, although most of the encounters mentioned in this book are real, I fictionalized some of the details and characters (minus two, Marie and Pete, who wanted their names in the book) to protect their identities.

2

AGING

Aging is a relevant issue in any time, place, and culture. According to the Bible, after the Fall recorded in Genesis 3, aging toward death became a reality for the human race. Here is the view of aging from the book of Ecclesiastes 12:1–8:

> ^{1}Remember your Creator in the days of your youth,
>> before the days of trouble come
>>> and the years approach when you will say, "I find no pleasure in them"—
>> ^{2}before the sun and the light and the moon
>>> and the stars grow dark,
>>> and the clouds return after the rain;
>> ^{3}when the keepers of the house tremble,
>>> and the strong men stoop,
>> when the grinders cease because they are few,
>>> and those looking through the windows grow dim;
>> ^{4}when the doors to the street are closed
>>> and the sound of grinding fades;

when men rise up at the sound of birds,

   but all their songs grow faint;

⁵when men are afraid of heights

   and of dangers in the streets;

when the almond tree blossoms

   and the grasshopper drags himself along

   and desire no longer is stirred.

Then man goes to his eternal home

   and mourners go about the streets.

⁶Remember him—

   before the silver cord is severed,

   or the golden bowl is broken;

   before the pitcher is shattered at the spring,

   or the wheel broken at the well,

      ⁷and the dust returns to the ground it came from, and the spirit returns to God who gave it.

⁸"Meaningless! Meaningless!" says the Teacher. "Everything is meaningless!"

In this final section (11:9–12:8) of Ecclesiastes, the author is summing up the entire book, concluding the treatise in poetic fashion where human experience ends— old age and death. He wants his readers to live in a two-fold awareness of God as the Creator (12:1) and Judge (11:9). In order to impress the urgency of his counsel on his reader's (hearer's) mind, the author paints a vivid and symbolic picture of the physiological, psychosocial, and spiritual decay occurring as we age and face death (12:1–8). The themes are highly metaphorical, likening the human body and process of aging to everyday things and events in the ancient Near Eastern world. After carefully detailing the trials of old age, the author concludes the extended word picture by describing the cessation of earthly life altogether, and the separation of the soul from the aged body (12:7).

According to the ancient teacher, the aging body is like a house entering into a state of disrepair. Hair turns white. Arms and legs develop weakness and tremors. Musculoskeletal deformities occur and walking becomes difficult. Teeth rot out, lips sink into the mouth, and food is "gummed" rather than chewed. Problems with eyesight develop. Worries and anxieties trouble the mind, resulting in light sleep and critical moods. Sexual impotence occurs. Suffering and loss are experienced, and at every moment death is just around the corner—the "silver cord" is ready to be snapped, and the "golden bowel" is set to be broken. The biblical picture of aging pulls no punches, but it is true to human experience because of the Fall (see chapter six).

Medical Science, the Bible, and Aging

Ecclesiastes describes what happens when we age, but it provides limited insight when we seek to understand how we age. God has blessed us with advances in medical science to help us answer some of these questions. Medical science informed by the Bible provides insight into the mechanisms occurring behind aging, and they teach us about how we age.

On the microscopic level, cells are constantly dying in our bodies and new cells emerge. For example, our body replaces its skin (epithelial cells) once a month. Estimates suggest that older adults have 30 percent fewer cells than in youth. Also at the cellular level, a decrease in intra- and extracellular fluids occur as we age. Total bodily fluid decreases, making older adults susceptible to dehydration. There are also anatomical and physiological changes caused by aging, not disease processes. God created the human body to be constantly working toward homeostasis (i.e., balance), through a congeries of internal and external biological, psychological, spiritual, and social factors, but after the Fall this balance was interfered with, and every bodily system down to the microscopic level ages and experiences the debilitating effects of aging.

Aging: Musculoskeletal System

The importance of mobility and functional activity cannot be overstated. One of the first systems affected by aging is the musculoskeletal system. In order for this system to sustain itself appropriate levels of activity are required, rest is needed, and adequate nourishment is necessary. The major contributors to a loss of functional status are a decrease in muscle mass, loss of strength, and decline in skeletal rigidity. Only 27 percent of the older adult population is regularly active, and this inactivity decreases muscle use and causes deterioration. One of the earliest signs of aging is musculoskeletal changes, such as muscle wasting, flabbiness, changes in posture, and lack of mobility in the joints.

As we age, our muscles atrophy (i.e., waste away). This process begins around forty. As our muscles waste, fibrous tissue forms and non-regenerating muscle cells die. It becomes more difficult to control bodily movements due to lack of muscle, and older adults become more easily fatigued when moving.

Also around forty, bone mass and density start to decline, leading to possible fractures (e.g., hip fractures are the most common). Women are more vulnerable to bone loss, losing two inches in height to the man's one. At thirty, the joints start to deteriorate, and by seventy, these complex hinges have experienced a life's worth of wear and tear.

Five major marks of aging in the musculoskeletal system are wasting of muscles, lack of strength, loss of agility, decreased endurance, and increased fatigue.

Aging: Neurocognitive System

The effects of aging on the neurological system are difficult to ascertain because of its close association with other systems and neurocognitive problems with similar signs. Perhaps the only way to distinguish aging from an acute neurocognitive process is the older adult's ability to recover. The major effect of aging on the neurological system is non-recoverable brain shrinkage, which causes a loss of neurons (gray-and-white matter in the brain), resulting in impaired thinking, decreased motor skills, and diminished sensory function. Irreversible cell loss in the brain begins around fifty, and cognitive, motor, and proprioceptive deficits follow.

We interact with the environment around us via our nervous system. The nervous system organizes data and it communicates with the world around us by receiving, processing, and responding to information at an incredible speed. As we age, it takes longer to think and respond, which is why older adults need more time to process information.

The nervous system is also responsible for our voluntary and involuntary muscle movements. The aging neurological system causes the older adult to move more slowly, and this affects his or her ability to drive, write, and dress, among other tasks taken for granted when younger.

Proprioception is the sense of one's position, posture, and equilibrium; it is a complex system providing the body with homeostasis necessary for survival. The neurological system is constantly adjusting our bodies unconsciously to maintain balance, temperature, blood pressure, etc. The brain interacting with the mind is responsible for these neurocognitive functions, and as the brain shrinks with aging, neurons die, and irreversible deficits follow.

Aging: Respiratory and Circulatory Systems

Good respiratory health may be the difference between an active and passive lifestyle for the older adult. Older adults who experience shortness of breath or the subjective feeling of breathlessness will not engage in activities and will remain sedentary, and this leads to quicker aging and deterioration of the body.

Aging reduces the older adult's breathing capacity, and by ninety most lungs have enough alveolar (the sacks in the lungs that exchange carbon dioxide and oxygen) damage to classify for a diagnosis of chronic obstructive pulmonary disease (COPD). Other changes occurring in the respiratory system with aging are structural: enlargement of the ribcage (barrel chest), stiffening of the intercostal muscles (elastic muscles between the ribs), kyphosis (hunchback), and a reduced elasticity of the lungs. These structural problems prevent full expansion of the lungs in older adults. The best defense against the effects of aging is to practice good respiratory health—stay away from cigarettes, perform deep breathing exercises, and maintain the highest level of functioning possible.

The effects of aging on the cardiovascular system are also well known, but it is difficult to determine whether these problems result from aging or underlying disease. Heart disease is the leading cause of chronic disease and death for people over fifty, and cardiac impairment is a major cause of functional decline. Several changes occur in the heart and blood vessels as people age. Atherosclerosis (progressive thickening of the wall inside the artery by calcium, collagen, or lipid deposits) starts immediately following birth. The arteries, vessels carrying oxygen rich blood from the heart to the body, are pliable and elastic when young, but as we age, the vessels become worn, elongated, narrow, lose their elasticity, and they become more easily clogged, especially if the older adult is not eating a proper diet and exercising. These obstructions cause the heart to work harder and prevent adequate blood flow to the organs and extremities.

The heart is a muscular organ that requires electrical conduction to pump. As the heart ages, muscle fibers become tough and non-elastic, thus, the heart's ability to contract, push blood out, and fill-up becomes impaired. A condition called cardiomyopathy may occur, which leads to heart failure. Cardiologists estimate that cardiac output decreases by 50 percent in people over eighty.

Other problems associated with aging on the heart are the thickening of heart valves leading to ineffective closing (causing a heart murmur). Hypertension (elevated blood pressure) is the most common problem in the older adult population, affecting roughly 70 percent of the American population over seventy-five. The conduction pathways also become impaired with age, leading to a heart that beats to slow or fast.

The aging heart, with the lungs running a close second, is the leading cause for inactivity and rapidity in aging in the older adult population.

Aging: Psychosocial and Spiritual Factors
Biological results from aging are significant, but equally noteworthy are psychosocial and spiritual factors. When God created us, he placed within us an innate need to be dependent upon his creation, his creatures, and ultimately

upon him to live a full and vibrant life. A cursory read of Genesis 1 and 2 identifies five basic needs we possess: (1) physiological and bodily needs, (2) protection and security needs, (3) love and companionship needs, (4) sanctification and mastery needs, and (5) the need for contentment. In the pre-Fall condition, Adam and Eve fulfilled these needs with perfect dependence on God, the creation, and one another. After Adam and Eve turned away from their Creator, unsatisfied needs started to whittle away at our lifespan, self-survival shifted to the center, and the fulfillment of these needs became an object of devotion.

Prior to creating humans, God made the world conducive to human existence, and provided the necessary nutrients and means to sustain and propagate human life. God created Adam and Eve from part of the earth, and, therefore, dependent on the earth. He breathed into them life (a life force or soul), and, therefore, made them dependent upon him. The human body must fulfill basic earth bound needs to survive and maintain homeostasis, such as breathe air, drink water, eat food, sleep, and engage in sex to propagate the human race. When these needs are not satisfied, illness, stress, anxiety, fear, pain, alienation, loss of joy, discomfort, and eventually death will come. These physiological and bodily drives are innate (unconsciously at work in us to motivate us), and in the older adult population, inability to fulfill these most basic needs (ability to breath, drink, eat, and sleep) will increase human suffering and quickly tear days off the calendar of life.

After creating Adam and Eve, God placed them together unclothed in a lush garden among the animals; there was no fear or shame—they felt secure. God created humans with an innate desire to feel safe, unthreatened, and protected. Today satisfaction of this need may mean feeling secure at home among family, and possessing adequate financial resources to live. In the older adult population, the ability to fulfill this need is a significant problem. The older adult becomes more dependent on others, and financial resources become quickly depleted. The desire to feel secure may have a positive effect by driving the older adult to seek help, security in God, membership at a local church, and assistance from local agencies, or it can drive the person to further alienation, despair, depression, and even suicide. Feeling safe, un-threatened, and secure is not only a legal right; it is an innate need God wants us to fulfill.

God created humans with a need for one another's love and companionship. He created Eve for Adam with this very purpose in mind, but even prior to this, God was a companion to Adam. We possess an innate need to feel loved and to live in loving relationships with others. One of the most special and intimate relationships in this world is marriage—a holistic relationship shared with a person of the opposite sex. The need for love relates closely to security because there is a sense of belonging and acceptance in love. In the older adult population, marriages, some over fifty years, terminate in the death of a spouse. Loss is nearly a daily occurrence for the older adult, and this may lead to bitterness, isolation, depression, and suicide (see chapter six). The worst possible thing an older adult can do is deny the need for love, because that means he or she will not seek to love others by entering into relationships with them.

Humans possess an intrinsic need to mature and master life. After God created Adam and Eve, he instructed them to rule over the creation and their own lives, underneath his authority in worshipful devotion to him. For older adults losing independence, this drive may become an immature desire to control anything possible, even if it is detrimental to one's health, safety, and well-being (such as driving a car when a healthcare provider revokes a driver's license for a medical reason). In older adult years, the time has come to share strategies on how to live successfully with the younger generation, while reminiscing about the past lived for the glory of God.

This leads to the final need, which is contentment with God's will or providence in life. Contentment frames the entire creation account. It was when Adam and Eve expressed discontentment with the Creator and his design for life that our God given needs became the very means to harm us, lead us astray, shorten our lifespans, and cause us to age.

Biological, psychosocial, and spiritual factors converge when people age to cause increased rapidity in aging. The anatomical and physiological effects associated with aging occur at every level of the human person. Changes occur in the musculoskeletal, neurocognitive, respiratory, and cardiovascular systems. Every major system of the body experiences the effects of aging down to the microscopic level. Since the Fall aging affects everyone; but there are things the older adult can do to live healthy at present to age well, even while on the aging trajectory to death—a topic we will turn to next.

3

HEALTHY
LIVING

We live in a day of unprecedented advances in disease prevention, nutrition, and healthy living. We know more about the human body today than any other time in history. Yet, it is also important to remember, the knowledge we possess is not without error. Recently, I read *The South Beach Diet* by Dr. Arthur Agatston (a cardiologist by specialty), and he pointed out that the diet recommended by the American Heart Association for years was actually detrimental to heart health. We have more knowledge about healthy living today than yesteryear, but we still have a lot to learn. Nevertheless, God expects us to use the most up to date knowledge we have to help us live healthy lives today.

In the last chapter, we looked at the inescapable effects of aging, now we will study how a healthy lifestyle helps the older adult age well with the time God grants.

The Struggle to Live Healthy

The expectation mentioned above, transcends every time in history, reaching back to the beginning. In the Garden of Eden, the Creator told Adam, Eve, and the human race to rule over the creation under his guidance (see Gen. 1:28 and 2:19–20). This mandate included caring for one's own body according to the light given by the Creator. This may sound overly simplistic, but caring for one's body means listening to the body in light of the Creator's revelation—a task more easily accomplished before the Fall.

For example, my stomach growls, so it is time to eat. My stomach is full, so it is time to stop eating. Due to the Fall, however, we have a tendency to go to extremes. A person absorbed with self-image refuses to eat and becomes anorexic, and another consumed with self-pity eats gluttonously and becomes obese. In every time and age, the Creator expects us to care for our bodies, mainly, by listening carefully to them, and by responding biblically to the messages sent by them.

How to Live a Healthy Life

Older adults can delay, and even prevent chronic conditions; such as heart disease, arthritis, stroke, some types of cancer and adult onset diabetes by living healthy lives. Physically active older adults eating a balanced diet, avoiding tobacco products, and following recommended medical screenings will reduce their risk of chronic diseases. In fact, older adults living healthy lifestyles experience only one-half the long-term illnesses of non-healthy people and disabilities due to aging do not occur until seven to ten years later.

In order to strive toward the goal of healthy living, we will cover several areas the older adult needs to address for a healthy life to occur. The first of these is healthy behaviors, which has moderation and thanksgiving at their cornerstone. We need to re-learn how to listen to our bodies in light of Scripture, and how to give God thanks for his many blessings. Next, we will consider nutrition, vitamins, and supplements for the older adult. Then, we will move on to study the older adult and exercise, and consider the important component of sleep. We will look at eye, foot, and skin care for the older adult; and vaccines older adults need as a defense against harmful microorganisms. Finally, we will conclude with a brief look at dental care. God willing, this information will help the older adult live a healthy life, even as aging takes its toll.

Moderation and Thanksgiving
Living a healthy life is part of the sanctification process in the Christian life, which means drawing near to God in

holy living. By God's empowering grace, we need to lay aside sinful desires, renew our thinking according to the Bible, and continuously put on the desires of the new person in Jesus Christ (Eph. 4:22–24). This is not just one-half of the person either (soul), but the whole person as a unit (soul-body). Sanctification is a process of renewal in the "whole man," as the Westminster Shorter Catechism says, leading on to a glorified resurrection of the body and soul at the second coming of Christ.

Unfortunately, a thread of Platonic thought has weaved its way into the fabric of the church's understanding of the human person today, and this has led to a neglect of the body. The philosopher Plato taught that the body was like a prison that held the soul captive. In Plato's thought, the soul was all that mattered, and the sooner the body died and set the soul free the better. Many of the early church fathers adopted Plato's teaching and this has led to extreme forms of the asceticism in Roman Catholic and Orthodox churches, and more recently to the evangelical focus on "saving souls" rather than the whole person. The Bible sees the human person as a body-soul unit, and any view of sanctification that does not keep the body and soul together as a unit is not rooted in Scripture.

While everyone is able to listen to his or her body, Christians have the ability to tune in to their bodies according to the will of God, as revealed in the Bible. This means, we should seek to develop the habit of listening to our bodies, by repeatedly asking ourselves: "What is my body telling me?" This question needs to become innate in us, so that we hear our bodies unconsciously. Proverbs is one book among many in the Bible that is full of advice for wise living, exhorting us repeatedly to listen to our bodies. We are to stop eating when satiated (25:16), stop drinking alcohol when the effects of intoxication are felt (23:20), treat bodily pain when it occurs (31:6), etc. As we seek to lay aside the old person, renew our mind, and put on the new person, we need to listen to our body in light of God's revelation to guide us in healthy living.

Due to the desires of the old man, however, it is possible to hear what the body is saying but ignore its messages. In this instance, we need to deny our desire to disobey. One of the fruits the Spirit produces in Christians is "self-control" (Gal. 5:23). Christians are to say no to overindulgent desires, by living in obedience to the spiritual fruit of self-control.

While it is always sinful to give into our desires to overindulge, it may be just as sinful to practice abstinence if it leads to a prideful or self-righteous attitude. We may need to practice abstinence to refrain from abusing substances that have a tendency to control us or to prevent ill health, but continued abstinence is not necessarily the biblical answer; especially if one is sinning by being prideful or self-righteous because of his or her abstinence!

"For everything God created is good," Paul wrote, "and nothing is to be rejected if it is received with thanksgiving" (1 Tim. 4:4). In this section in Paul's letter to Timothy, Paul is essentially saying, if we do not delight ourselves in the blessings of the creation, we may show a spirit of ingratitude toward the Creator. I love Jonathan Edwards's comment on this topic, to paraphrase; we bring God glory when we delight ourselves fully in all of his creation. This does not give us license to abuse the creation, but it encourages us to enjoy all of it with thanksgiving.

> So I recommend the enjoyment of life, for there is nothing better on earth for a person to do except to eat, drink, and enjoy life. So joy will accompany him in his toil during the days of his life which God gives him on earth. (Eccles. 8:15, NET)

The writer of Ecclesiastes encourages the reader to flee the ascetic life, and to enjoy the blessings God has given, even in the midst of life's difficulties. John Calvin in the *Golden Booklet of the True Christian Life* provides these insightful words: "the use of [the] gifts of God cannot be wrong, if they are directed to the same purpose for which the Creator himself created and destined them."

Listening to our body according to the light God has given us, avoiding extremes, exercising moderation, displaying the fruit of self-control, and expressing gratitude to the Creator for his creation, is living the full-orbed sanctified life here and now. These behaviors will help the older adult prevent health problems, promote healthy living, and increase joy.

Diet, Nutrition, and Supplements

Advances in diet and nutrition have increased our ability to live healthy lives. Prior to the twentieth century, one could eat in moderation and listen carefully to the body, but still neglect ingesting necessary fats, amino acids, vitamins, and minerals. For example, scurvy a disease caused by the lack of vitamin C in one's diet, afflicted sailors on the high seas until the 1930s.

Today we have the ability to analyze food products to understand their nutritional content, as well as our body to determine the amounts of nutrients we need. Eating a well-balanced diet is important across the lifespan, but it is especially important for the older adult. Older adults eating an unbalanced diet are at an increased risk for heart disease, diabetes, stroke, immune deficiencies, osteoporosis, cancers, and overall poor health.

The older adult should avoid saturated fats and cholesterol, but be on the alert when using low- or non-fat foods. In low- or non-fat foods, the sugar content may be elevated to compensate for the lack of taste due to reduced fat. High sugar is worse than fat, and needs close monitoring. Although daily calorie counts differ from person to person, on average the active older adult female should eat around 2,200 calories a day, and the male around 2,800.

A well-balanced diet includes the following food groups and daily servings: unprocessed and non-enriched grains (one serving), fruits (one serving), vegetables (four servings), milk, yogurt, cheese (four servings), lean meat, poultry, fish, and nuts (one serving). Most food packages have a chart defining serving sizes, calories, and nutritional information. Part of a well-balanced diet is drinking at least eight cups (eight ounces) of water throughout the day.

The older adult eating a well-balanced diet will receive most of the necessary vitamins and minerals needed to live a healthy life, but some additional supplements may be helpful. A daily multivitamin is usually sufficient, but one's healthcare provider may perform a detailed diet and blood analysis to determine if specific deficiencies exist. It is not necessary to purchase the "senior" or brand name vitamins, the generic regular brands are sufficient. It is also important to report any vitamins or supplements to one's primary care provider, since they may interact with prescription medications.

Exercise and Fitness

After nutrition for the older adult, exercise is the most important behavior for healthy living. The National Institute on Aging reported that lack of exercise was the second leading underlying cause of chronic health problems leading to death in people over sixty-five. The report also said that the older adult is at a greater risk for health problems from lack of exercise, than potential injuries from engaging in exercise. The older adult remains active longer with exercise; and it helps to prevent heart disease, diabetes, colon cancer, and high blood pressure. All older adults should exercise at some level. If there are any health concerns, always talk to a healthcare provider before starting an exercise program.

The older adult's exercise regime should cover four areas. (1) Balance exercises (as often as possible), such as heel-toe walking, balancing on one foot, concentrating on balancing, etc., helps to prevent falls. (2) Endurance exercises (thirty minutes a day for six days), such as brisk walking, hiking, riding a bike, tennis, swimming, etc., helps to increase energy and stamina. If one is able to talk with no effort while exercising, then the activity is not vigorous enough. (3) Strengthening exercises (two to three times per week), such as lifting weights, resistance exercises, isometric exercises, mowing the lawn, etc., helps to build muscle and strengthen bones. (4) Stretching exercises (two to three times per week), such as muscle stretches without bouncing, range of motion, deep breathing, etc., helps to prevent stiffness, injury, stress, and increases flexibility.

Sleep and Rejuvenation

Sleeping well at night is part of healthy living. Yet, research indicates that more than 60 percent of the people over sixty-five have difficulty sleeping. These are usually not true sleep disorders, but underlying issues disturbing sleep. Several chronic medical conditions and medications will disturb sleep (see chapter six), but the major culprits behind sleep deprivation are years of submerged worry, stress, and unresolved grief. It is also in the quiet hours of the night the older adult faces his or her mortality without distraction. When King David lay awake at night he remembered God (Psa. 63:8), meditated on his promises (119:148), and this gave him peace.

One age-related problem connected to sleep deprivation is decreased rapid eye movement (REM) sleep. A reduction in REM sleep results in increased arousal during sleep, resulting in a decreased feeling of rejuvenation.

Normal sleep is broken up into two major segments: REM and non-REM sleep. Older adults with decreased REM sleep usually nap frequently during the day. As a result, they have difficulty falling asleep at night, wake up several times throughout the night, and feel fatigued after sleeping. The best way to manage decreased REM sleep is to develop a normal sleeping routine by going to bed at the same time each night, and denying oneself daytime naps.

Eyes, Feet, and Skin

As years take their toll on our body, we need to pay particular attention to our eyes, feet, and skin. Alteration in vision may have a profound effect on a healthy lifestyle. Visual disturbances affect the older adult's ability to ambulate and read information, making him or her more susceptible to injuries (see chapter six).

When I think of two areas on the body that take a beating, I think of the feet and skin. The older adult has stepped on his or her feet for more than half a century. Proper foot care may mean the difference between a sedentary and active lifestyle. The skin is the first line organ system interacting with the environment around us. As we age, our skin becomes thinner, spots develop, wrinkles appear, dryness occurs, and it takes longer to heal when injured. Not to mention, 50 percent of the older adult population will develop skin cancer at least once in his or her lifetime. Good foot and skin care are necessary components to living a healthy life.

Vaccines

Since the introduction of the smallpox vaccine in the eighteenth century, vaccines have come a long way. Jonathan Edwards, one of America's premier theologians from the eighteenth century, died after an inoculation for smallpox, but today we never hear of cases of smallpox in the United States. Since the eighteenth century, vaccinations have become a safe and effective means to eradicate disease. Today's vaccines no longer use the active virus or bacterium (which is what killed Edwards) but an attenuated, or weakened, form of it. The healthy immune system is able to overcome the attenuated virus or bacterium and develop resistance to it. The benefits of vaccines significantly outweigh the risks, which is why the federal government mandates specific vaccines for children to protect them and prevent the spread of diseases.

Vaccines are not just for children, but the Center for Disease Control (CDC) recommends specific vaccinations and boosters for the older adult. More than 36,000 people die from the flu each year, but less than 65 percent of the older adult population receives the flu vaccine. Statistics show that the flu vaccine reduces hospitalizations by 27 percent, and it reduces the death rate by one-half. Pneumonia is a serious health problem in the older adult population as well. People over sixty-five should receive a one-time dose of the pneumococcal vaccine as well. The CDC also recommends the chickenpox vaccine for older adults who did not have the chicken pox, and the organization recommends a booster for tetanus and diphtheria every ten years.

Dental Care

The older we get, the more we appreciate our teeth. Like our feet and skin, our teeth experience years of use and often neglect. Often we do not brush, floss, and have regular cleanings. As a result, older adults require expensive dental work after retirement (when work-assisted dental policies have ceased). The dental problems for older adults, such as dental caries, oral cancer, and gingival disease, are the same as any other stage of life. Problems with dentures are unique to the older adult population, however. After one receives dentures, it is still necessary to visit the dentist to evaluate for oral cancer and to assess the fit, function, and wear of the dentures. Dental care is usually available for older adults at reduced rates at public clinics and dental schools.

Living a healthy life is a God-honoring life, for it is the sanctified life. Through Christ's work of redemption, Christians are able to listen to their body according the light God has given, and are empowered by the Holy Spirit to avoid extremes by manifesting the fruit of self-control. As the older adult walks after Jesus in gratitude, this holy life will help to prevent chronic health problems, and promote a full-orbed life of sanctification—body and soul—leading on to glorification at Jesus' second coming. As the older adult learns how to listen to his or her body in light of Scripture, thanksgiving and gratitude will overflow, and the healthy life will create a new-found excitement in obeying the creation mandate, especially as he or she enjoys God's creation fully. Having looked at how to live a healthy God honoring life, next we will move on to consider the application of preventive healthcare.

4

PREVENTIVE
HEALTHCARE

One of the benefits for most Americans turning sixty-five is the ability to participate in Medicare, a federally funded health insurance program taxes supplement. The program is broken down into four policies labeled A, B, C, and D. Medicare part A is hospital insurance. B is medical insurance (usually outpatient services). Medicare Advantage is C (a policy arranged with a private insurer with A, B, other special benefits, and drug coverage). Medicare Prescription Drug Coverage is D (this is a policy arranged through a private insurer providing coverage for medications). The cost of each policy varies depending on the arrangement, but if a person paid Medicare taxes, part A has no monthly premium, and part B has a minimum ninety-nine dollar a month premium. Once enrolled in Medicare, the policy has a yearly open season for modification (each year the Centers for Medicare & Medicaid Services (CMMS) publishes *Medicare & You* [www.medicare.gov], a guide outlining specific policy changes and coverage. I refer the reader to this guide for detailed information).

Medicare came into existence in 1965 under Title XVIII of the Social Security Act. Initially, Congress established Medicare to provide healthcare for people over sixty-five regardless of medical history or income. The original intent was to offer underprivileged older adults with no health insurance (which were most retired Americans) with access to adequate medical care. In 1972, Congress expanded Medicare to provide coverage for younger people with disabilities and those with end-stage kidney disease. Then in 2001, another expansion occurred to include citizens with Lou Gehrig's disease (amyotrophic lateral sclerosis or ALS).

According to the latest statistics, Medicare covered forty-eight million Americans, forty million were sixty-five and older and eight million were under sixty-five; the program paid out $560 billion. Projections indicate that by 2030, recipients of Medicare will increase to eighty million (almost double), and by 2022 the cost to Medicare will exceed one trillion dollars. A government-driven humanitarian program originally created to serve the older adult population has exploded into a huge fiscal burden for the government and the taxpayer, and today it is one of the most hotly debated programs on Capitol Hill.

The Affordable Care Act (ACA)

In an attempt to address this burden, president Obama established the Patient Protection and Affordable Care Act (PPACA, now known as the Affordable Care Act [ACA] or Obamacare) on March 23, 2010. The ACA will come into full effect by 2014, and the changes are sweeping to America's healthcare system. Rather than consider the entire act, I will limit myself to those changes directly affecting the older adult.

Title III of the Act will establish more efficient, effective, and patient-centered medical care by providing incentives to healthcare personnel and institutions for fiscal responsibility. Underneath this same title, Medicare recipients will receive new preventive medical benefits to improve overall health, and the Medicare D program will become more affordable by closing the gap known as the "donut hole."

Title VI of the Act requires transparency. Pharmaceutical and medical technology companies need to report gifts given to physicians on a public website. This title also requires transparency in the nursing home industry, by providing information about skilled nursing and rehabilitative care facilities.

Title IX creates new taxes on higher-income wage earners, drug companies, medical device companies, and private health insurance providers. These taxes will help to pay specifically for Medicare.

One proposal that was not included in the ACA was Section 1233 of bill HR 3200 and this was unfortunate. This provision would have reimbursed physicians for providing counseling to Medicare recipients about living wills, advance directives, and end-of-life care decisions. In 2009, Sarah Palin caused a stir when she called the proposal a "death panel" provision. According to the vice president hopeful, HR 3200 would have created a policy where public officeholders decide who is worthy of government funding for medical care. Ultimately, according to Palin, the government will determine who lives or dies. Some conservative pundits ran with the claim, blowing it out of proportion. Due to public unrest over the issue, Congress removed the provision from the final version of the ACA, and this move was unfortunate for older adults.

HR 3200 may be a concern in states where physician-assisted suicide (PAS) is legal and end-of-life counseling may include this option. One should not throw out the baby with the bath water, however. Medicare as a whole needs a provision like this because it helps older adults make informed decisions about expensive medical care they usually do not want, but when unresponsive due to an injury or sickness, have to receive. HR 3200 would not have created death panels where bureaucrats decide; rather, it would have helped older adults make informed decisions to prevent futile medical intervention, and it would have saved Medicare thousands if not millions of dollars.

In 2010, *60 Minutes* aired "The Cost of Dying" and reported that in 2009 alone Medicare "paid $50 billion just for doctor and hospital bills during the last two months of patients' lives." According to the program, this exceeded the spending for the Department of Homeland Security that year. The *60 Minutes* correspondent also reported that the daily average cost for a bed in an intensive care unit (ICU) is $10,000 and 20 to 30 percent of the people on Medicare treated in ICUs that year had no benefit from the treatment. HR 3200 would have helped older adults plan wisely, it would not have created "death panels."

The other incentives for preventive medical care in the ACA are already in the *Medicare & You* handbook. Medicare as governed by the ACA focuses on disease prevention to reduce healthcare costs and to enhance a healthy lifestyle. The *Medicare & You* handbook provides a comprehensive checklist created by physicians for preventive health screening; the manual urges Medicare recipients to review the checklist with their primary care provider every year. Any tests the provider deems necessary are covered. Another benefit is a yearly wellness visit free of charge, aimed at helping the older adult live a healthy lifestyle.

Although controversial (and perhaps not even sustainable), the changes to Medicare the ACA implements support the older adult seeking to prevent chronic diseases by creating incentives, guidance, and tools for the Medicare recipient to live responsibly.

The Older Adult's Healthcare Team

One of the key elements to healthy aging and disease prevention is the creation of a healthcare team. Aside from the older adult, family members, and local church, the primary member on the care team is the healthcare provider. This is usually the family doctor, but he or she may not be the best professional for the older adult at this stage of life. When transitioning to Medicare, it may be wise to switch to a healthcare provider specializing in geriatric care (or to a provider who focuses on caring for Medicare patients).

Geriatrician

A geriatrician is a physician or a nurse practitioner specializing in the care of people sixty-five and over, which means he or she received additional education, training, and certification in caring for the older adult population.

There are several advantages to having a geriatrician rather than a general practitioner. Foremost, a geriatrician chooses to specialize in the care of older adults. This means he or she is more likely to subscribe to geriatric journals, attend conferences aimed at caring for people over sixty-five, and stay up-to-date on issues affecting the older adult population. The geriatrician also has a greater awareness of disease conditions specific to the older adult, subtle side effects of medications for geriatric patients, and a better understanding of the unique psychosocial needs the older adult population faces. Typically, geriatricians spend more time with patients. This means older adults are better able to process information, voice concerns, and ask questions. Finally, geriatricians are equipped to focus on the entire older person, and his or her living situation; rather than a disease process, and a large spectrum of people across the lifespan.

When choosing a provider, the older adult should answer the following questions to his or her satisfaction: Does the provider explain things clearly in nonprofessional terms, talk about difficult issues, and regularly review medications? What are the provider's religious connections, beliefs, and morals? Does the provider visit nursing homes, rehabilitation centers, hospitals, and make home visits? Does the provider offer preventive medical teaching and instruction on advance directives?

Does the provider advertise supportive services, such as eldercare services? Is the office staff friendly, engaging, and helpful? Answering the following questions will help to identify an adequate provider, preferably one who is a geriatrician.

Pharmacist

While I was at CVS the other day, I saw an elderly couple approach a busy pharmacist to ask her which cough syrup to buy. The pharmacist stopped what she was doing, asked them about the symptoms, and recommended the proper cough syrup. A pharmacist is another important team member for the older adult. The pharmacist possesses knowledge about medications, problems relating to specific types of medications, appropriate usage and dosage, drug interactions, adverse effects, and information on generic and discounted drugs. The geriatrician and pharmacist are two major team members for the older adult, but the older adult will find other important team members at church and in the local community.

Eldercare Services

Most communities have eldercare services geared toward preventive healthcare. In the community I live, the organization is the Council on Aging. The group is well structured and is very active in the community, providing education, advocacy, services, and social interaction for people sixty-five and over. Aside from in home assistance, other major services Council on Aging provides are Meals on Wheels, adult daycare and senior center programs, transportation, and a website with a plethora of information for older adults and caregivers. A board of directors governs the organization, but it also has fulltime staff and volunteers. Council on Aging receives funds through federal and local grants, as well as donations from individuals and businesses. This is an excellent resource, but the older adult's church should be the primary supporter for care.

Church

Historically, aside from one's family, the church was the place to go to for healing, assistance, and hope. With the advent of modern medicine, our pluralistic culture has pushed churches aside and put medical institutions and government-funded programs in their place. Unfortunately, many Christians have adopted this mindset, and now they merely look to churches for social networking, feel-good entertainment, inspirational messages, and an exciting "otherworldly" experience. Tragically, many list going to church alongside other activities like playing golf or shopping. This view of the church is not correct.

In the early church, the picture was not one of selfish pleasure but selfless commitment, sharing, and caring, especially to the "aged." The local church was central, not peripheral to one's life. Christians devoted themselves to the apostle's doctrine, worship, fellowship, and prayer on a daily basis (see Acts 4:42–47). Believers united with one another in a spirit of humility, gentleness, patience, forbearance, and love (Eph. 4:4). Love and care for one another was the mark of a vibrant and growing church. "People will know that you are my disciples," said Jesus, "if you have love for one another" (John 13:35). The love Christians show to one another reflects Jesus' love for them. Paul exhorts believers with this carefully crafted statement:

> If you have any encouragement from being united with Christ, if any comfort from his love, if any fellowship with the Spirit, if any tenderness and compassion, then make my joy complete by being like-minded, having the same love, being one in spirit and purpose. Do nothing out of selfish ambition or vain conceit, but in humility consider others better than yourselves. Each of you should look not only to your own interests, but also to the interests of others. (Phil. 2:1–4)

Paul is saying, if you have experienced the patience, gentleness, humility, kindness, and compassion of Christ, all facets of Jesus' love (which all Christians experience), then reciprocate these character traits to others.

In the apostolic church, believers cared for one another with practical acts of mercy based upon their love for Christ. For example, they fed, clothed, visited, and took care of one another when sick. In Paul's letter to the Philippians, there is a moving account of Paul's loving concern for his sick companion Epaphroditus. He writes to the church at Philippi, "Indeed he was ill, and almost died. But God had mercy on him, and not on him only but also on me, to spare me sorrow upon sorrow" (Phil. 2:27). Jesus even went so far to say that selfless care for fellow Christians is an indicator of whether a person will go to heaven (Matt. 25:31–46).

The Bible is replete with exhortations to care for older adults, especially one's parents. The fifth commandment says, "Honor your father and your mother" (Exod. 20:12). In the immediate context, the commandment refers to devotion to one's biological parents but by extension, it refers to any older adult member in the church—a spiritual parent. John has this in mind when he writes in poetic form about spiritual relationships in the church, "I write to you, fathers," that is, those older men in the church (1 John 2:13). Jesus also refers to familial ties that are spiritual when he says, "'Who is my mother, and who are my brothers?' Pointing to his disciples, he said, 'Here are my mother and my brothers . . . whoever does the will of my Father in heaven is my brother and sister and mother'" (Matt. 12:48–50). Scripture is clear; Christians have a duty to biological parents, but they also have a responsibility to care for older adults in their churches.

Pastors, Elders, Deacons, and Healers

All Christians need to care for older adults in their midst in practical ways, but a special duty rests on pastors, elders, deacons, and those with the post-apostolic gift of healing. Pastors and elders provide biblical insight into ethical questions about medical care, psychological and spiritual counseling, and prayerful intercession on behalf of the older adult. Deacons evaluate the mercy needs for older adults by organizing and implementing the practical aspects of ministry. Christians with the post-apostolic gift of healing are those who work in the healthcare field and are members of a congregation. These doctors, nurses, social workers, and other healthcare workers do not possess the apostolic gift of healing (i.e., the power to miraculously heal people), but they are gifted because God has blessed them with the ability to understand and apply the art and science of professional medical care. The older adult, pastor, elders, and deacons may look to these healers for advice, wisdom, and guidance on healthcare matters.

Congregational Nurses

Churches with a large older adult population may benefit from a congregational nurse or parish nurse program, which is technically a type of diaconal ministry. In Acts 6:1–7, the apostles chose seven men to care for the needy in the church, and these men were deacons. Years later Paul wrote to Timothy at the church in Ephesus and gave specific instructions on how to choose people for diaconal work (1 Tim. 3:8–13). Throughout the New Testament and ancient church era, we read about men and women performing duties of stewardship and mercy for members of the church. Widows served the congregation through practical acts of ministry (1 Tim. 5:3–16), and a woman named Phoebe was praised by Paul for her service as a "deaconess" (Rom. 16:1–2). Diaconal ministry and nursing run tandem in the early church because historically they were really the same ministry.

In fact, nursing as a profession has its roots in diaconal ministry not Western medicine. Medicine seeks to diagnose and treat diseases that afflict the body, and this finds it origin in Greek philosophy (i.e., naturalism) and Hippocrates of Cos, not the Bible. Nursing, on the other hand, seeks to identify and care for the needs of the whole person (body and soul) in his or her diseased, traumatized, or dying state, and this finds its root in the diaconal ministry of the church. The parable of the Good Samaritan shows what this type of care looks like in action (see Luke 10:30–35).

Diaconal nursing care is compassionate in focus, sacrificial in giving, and preventive in aim. These caregivers are intimately involved with the afflicted, providing comfort, safety, and palliation of symptoms. The congregational nurse functions as a healthcare advocate and primary care resource for older adults. He or she serves as a liaison between the pastor, elders, deacons, congregation, geriatrician, other healthcare professionals, and community, ensuring the older adult receives adequate healthcare. The congregational nurse will visit older adults to assess medical, psychosocial, and spiritual needs, and he or she will address those needs via resources in the church, the community, or both. Diaconal nurses educate older adults and families on preventing disease, medication management, and promoting health, and he or she helps to prepare documents to address end-of-life issues. The congregational nurse is really a deacon in the historical sense, one with the post-apostolic gift of healing, commissioned by the pastor, elders, and congregation to address the mercy needs of the church.

Practicing Preventive Healthcare

The older adult should see his or her healthcare provider at least once a year, and a newly enrolled Medicare recipient will want to bring the *Medicare & You* checklist to this visit. The following tips will help the older adult get the most out of visits. First, it is important to be open and honest with the provider. He or she is there to provide care, not to judge; so be frank and upfront with health concerns. Second, write out a list of questions before the visit and be sure to prioritize them (you may not have time to ask all of your questions). It may be helpful to bring someone along for support. Third, do not feel intimidated by the provider. If a word is confusing, ask for clarification. Also, tell the provider if money is an issue. If the provider orders treatments, medications, diagnostic tests, or makes a referral to a new specialist; make sure everything is in writing, and ask questions.

In between routine visits, the older adult should see his or her provider when the following signs or symptoms develop: a cold or flu accompanied by chest pain, shortness of breath, high fever, and productive cough lasting longer than two weeks. Contact the provider for nausea and vomiting lasting longer than two days, or if blood (may look like coffee grounds) is seen in the vomit. If the older adult develops a chronic fever (100 degrees Fahrenheit or greater), new bruises, or bleeding (nose, gums, or rectum), see the provider. The healthcare provider (or 911 depending on the severity) will require notification for a severe sudden headache, accompanied by other bodily changes such as numbness, dizziness, unsteady gait, speaking difficulties, facial drooping, or a stiff neck. When in doubt, it is always best to notify the healthcare provider right away if any new health problems develop.

When an older adult reports new signs or symptoms, one of the first things the provider will do is rule out medication as a cause. In 2010, the Food and Drug Administration (FDA) received over 90,000 reports for adverse drug reactions in the older adult population and 15,000 of these incidents were fatal. Medication is a primary suspect when new problems occur, but it is usually not the prescribed drug itself causing the problem. Rather, it is a combination of other things linked to the medication; like the older adult not taking the medication as prescribed, or an interaction with other prescribed medications, over-the-counter medications or supplements. Prescription medications are the mainstay for older adults with chronic disease conditions, but they also pose challenges—they need careful monitoring to practice preventive medicine effectively.

One primary challenge for medication compliance is cost. Over the course of a year, on average, the older adult pays about $2,500 for medications. This is roughly $208 a month, and most of the older adult population is on a fixed income. In the United States, half of the nation's prescribed pharmaceuticals are for older adults. Twenty-seven percent of Medicare recipients over sixty-five have no prescription drug benefit, which means they have to pay full cost for their medications. In light of these statistics, it is not surprising that more than one quarter of the older adult population is unable to fill their prescriptions due to an inability to pay. Cost is a major problem, but equally troublesome is unwanted side effects.

Adverse drug reactions are another major problem. Commonly prescribed medications for the older adult that can cause serious problems are warfarin (Coumadin), aspirin, digoxin, prednisone, diuretics (Lasix), anti-hypertensive agents, insulin, and psychotropic drugs. Another common problem with medications is drug-to-drug interactions. Older adults usually see a variety of specialists, and each of these physicians have a tendency to prescribe new medications. This is not only expensive and confusing to the older adult, but the medications may interact with one another.

Other adverse reactions occur when medications cause organ toxicity, or when diseased organs do not properly process medications. Also, eating certain foods, most notably grapefruit, may cause unwanted side effects with certain medications. All of these issues may cause adverse events, but the most common problems occur when prescribed medications interact with over-the-counter medications and supplements.

Medications purchased over the counter and supplements play a major role in the older adult population. Older adults purchase about 40 percent of all the over-the-counter medications in the United States. These medications treat pain, insomnia, and constipation, and, unknowingly, side effects from prescription medications! In the United States, about two million older adults invest in herbal and nutritional supplements as well. A major problem with natural supplements is many assume they have no adverse or toxic effects, and do not interact with medications because they are natural. On the contrary, many of these supplements interact with prescription medications, and may even be deadly. It is important for the older adult to report the use of over-the-counter medications and nutritional supplements to his or her provider.

The last problem concerning medications is non-compliance. If an older adult has to choose between buying food or a medication, he or she will probably choose the former—this is a form of non-compliance. Unfortunately, this behavior may have significant consequences for the older adult, because the mainstay for controlling chronic disease and practicing preventive healthcare is medication. According to an *Adult Meducation* report, medication non-compliance accounted for 10 percent of the hospital admissions in 2007 and one quarter of the nursing home admissions. Medication adherence issues resulted in 125,000 deaths that year, and the cost was $100 billion. Non-compliance is a significant issue, and the reasons behind it have very little to do with an attitude of defiance.

The primary way to overcome medication problems, and practice preventive healthcare is to adopt mechanisms and enlist people to ensure compliance with healthcare needs. Keeping open lines of communication is crucial for older adults to prevent medical problems, so older adults need to alert family members, church members, and primary care providers of any new health problems. During routine visits to one's healthcare provider, report on the effectiveness of prescribed medications, any side effects, and any new healthcare issues. Working with the healthcare provider, family, and church is a team effort, and along with Medicare, it is a good strategy for a robust preventive healthcare program.

Medicare is not a perfect program, but even with all its flaws, it is still a needed program for the older adult. If the government did not regulate the private sector, provide healthcare of its own, and offer private organizations grants to care for the less fortunate, the rich and upper middle class would have healthcare, and the poor and lower middle class would not. We would return to the pre-1965 state, and to a plethora of vulnerable senior citizens without adequate healthcare.

The ACA attempts to manage Medicare by providing preventive medical benefits for older adults, by adding higher standards of fiscal responsibility to healthcare providers, and by increasing taxes on higher wage earners. Every day I see literally thousands of dollars spent on futile procedures, ineffective surgeries, useless chemotherapy infusions, needless diagnostic testing, unused equipment—the list goes on. One major procedure and hospitalization quickly depletes an individual's lifetime tax investment into Medicare (even a higher wage earner's investment), never mind adding into the mix those who never worked or paid taxes to support the program at all.

Overall, the ACA advocates for the older adult seeking to live a responsible and healthy life. These goals are in accord with a biblical approach to healthcare, so Christians should welcome them and not fall prey to party politics. The ACA is also taking measures to help people with chronic disease conditions by closing the so-called "donut hole" and broadening the pharmaceutical market to lower the cost of medications to the older adult consumer. Under the ACA, older adults have the opportunity to create a formidable healthcare team for preventive healthcare, and now the next step is for the older adult to manage this healthcare wisely—a topic we will consider next.

5

HEALTHCARE MANAGEMENT

Jim was an eighty-three-year-old with Alzheimer's disease sent emergently to the hospital from a nursing home, after developing respiratory failure due to aspiration pneumonia (food or fluid entering the lungs). He had a breathing tube inserted into his throat, was placed on a ventilator, and received treatment in an ICU.

A neurologist diagnosed Jim with Alzheimer's disease six years prior, and his estranged son, Tony, became Jim's default healthcare proxy. Tony found placement for Jim at a nursing home shortly after diagnosis, and signed him up for Medicaid to pay for room and board at the facility. Jim's decline was relatively slow. After arriving at the nursing home, he was confused, but most of his functional abilities were still intact. At the time of admission to the hospital six years later, he was severely incapacitated. Jim was bedbound and non-responsive, and he required total care.

The hospital contacted Tony shortly after Jim's admission. Jim had no directives concerning aggressive treatment, so these decisions lay on Tony's shoulders. The last time Tony set eyes on Jim was about four years before the incident. Nevertheless, Tony refused to consent to a do-not-resuscitate order (DNRO), and he wanted everything done to prolong his father's life, even after the doctor gave his grim prognosis.

Two weeks after the admission, Tony received another call from the ICU. Jim was still non-responsive on the ventilator, but the temporary breathing and feeding tubes needed replacement with more permanent tubes. Tony had to give consent to cut a slit in Jim's throat to serve as an airway, and to puncture a hole in his abdomen to insert a feeding tube, which he did. A week following these procedures, Tony received another call because Jim's kidneys were shutting down and he needed dialysis; he gave consent for this procedure as well. Thirty-five days after admission to the hospital, Jim had a cardiac arrest, resuscitation techniques failed, and he died—Tony directed his father's care from miles away and never arrived at his bedside.

At seventy-six, a neurologist diagnosed Ruth with Alzheimer's disease. Two years prior, however, Ruth noticed lapses in her short-term memory, so she developed a long-term care strategy and drafted medical directives. Her daughter, Aria, agreed to care for Ruth as long as possible at her home, and Ruth chose a nursing home to go to if Aria could not handle her care. Ruth also made financial preparations to assist Aria, and to pay for her future room, board, and care at the nursing home. Ruth drafted healthcare directives that clearly stated she did not desire life-prolonging treatment, and she appointed Aria as her healthcare agent. In consultation with her geriatrician, Ruth signed a DNRO, and they discussed hospice care. Ruth chose a funeral home and spent time with her pastor preparing her funeral service. At the time of diagnosis, Ruth addressed as many needs as possible.

Ruth lived with Aria for six years before she could no longer care for her at the level she required. At this point, Ruth was bedbound, requiring frequent turning, and had incontinence. The geriatrician admitted Ruth to the nursing home of her choice and into a hospice program. Along with hospice support, Aria, the pastor, elders, deacons, and other church members visited on a regular basis. Ruth received excellent care, but like Jim, she developed aspiration pneumonia.

Ruth had a DNRO and advance healthcare directives declining aggressive life-prolonging treatment, so she remained at the nursing home. The nursing home notified Aria, the geriatrician, and the hospice of the decline in status, and the nurse administered medications to provide Ruth comfort. Soon the geriatrician arrived, as well as, her pastor, elders, deacons, and other members from church. The group sang hymns, drank coffee, reminisced, prayed, and fellowshipped around Ruth's bed until she fell asleep in Jesus several hours later.

Jim and Ruth had Alzheimer's disease, and the acute event that precipitated their decline was aspiration pneumonia, but their approach to healthcare was radically different. Ruth prepared ahead of time, and Jim did not. Jim's lack of preparation led to the appointment of his estranged son Tony, who was unrealistic about Jim's care. Jim's Alzheimer's disease was not going to get better, and Jim was in the last stages of the disease. Jim's care was not cheap. Aside from the daily cost for the nursing home from Medicaid, which was roughly $200 a day over six years ($432,000), the cost to Medicare for the ICU stay alone was $10,000 a day for thirty-five days ($350,000), never mind the treatments, procedures, medications, and plethora of specialists involved in his care—this hospitalization was futile and extremely expensive. On the other hand, Ruth prepared wisely and realistically for the days ahead; as a result, her experience had better quality and it was a lot cheaper ($160 a day for hospice care from Medicare).

In this chapter, we will consider crucial components for wise healthcare management, such as the Patient Self Determination Act (PSDA), guiding principles for Christians to consider when managing healthcare, advance healthcare directives, and life planning.

The Patient Self Determination Act (PSDA)

In 1990, Congress passed the Patient Self-Determination Act (PSDA). This act requires healthcare institutions and agencies receiving tax dollars to provide education, counseling, and documents for advance healthcare directives to their patients. The PSDA grants the adult patient or patient designee three rights: (1) the right to make his or her own healthcare decisions, (2) the right to accept or refuse medical treatments, and (3) the right to draft advance healthcare directives. Individual doctors were exempt from the PSDA for reimbursement purposes, which means they do not have to counsel people on advance directives. In the later 2010 ACA, however, HR 3200 would have tied physicians into the PSDA by providing them with reimbursement for counseling, but Palin's "death panel" scare laid this provision in the grave.

As illustrated above with Jim and Ruth, the PSDA is a two-edged sword. Although I do not care for the words "self-determination," the PSDA allows the older adult a way to manage and plan for his or her healthcare with God's glory in view. Three individuals can determine the course of medical treatment for the older adult: (1) the government, (2) the healthcare institution, and (3) the patient or designee. Personally, I prefer option three. The PSDA puts the patient in the driver's seat, the healthcare institution in the passenger seat, and the government in the back seat. Christians have the responsibility to care for their own bodies and take measures to alleviate potential burdens on others; the PSDA provides a way to accomplish these goals. "Self-determination" under the PSDA translates into the opportunity for the older adult to manage his or her healthcare wisely and responsibly, with the interests of his or her neighbors first, and the glory of God central.

Less than a century ago, careful management of one's healthcare was not a big issue. We did not have the life prolonging technology, procedures with questionable ethics, and the exorbitant costs we do today. Medical science was turning a corner seventy years ago, but it was still largely palliative in focus. Some people improved after treatment, some did not and died. In the 1960s, all of this changed with the treatment of death itself through cardiopulmonary resuscitation. Even if people did not improve after treatment, they could still live on life support. After the 1960s, medical science in the United States went on a rocket ride of change; fueled by a spirit of optimism with minimal government regulation, and funded by a seeming bottomless pit of newly created Medicare dollars. The result: enthusiastic doctors made unilateral decisions without patient consent, and taxpayers handled the cost. In 1990, Congress created the PSDA, which put the medical consumer in charge of managing his or her healthcare.

Guiding Principles for Managing Healthcare

The question naturally arises, "How should I manage my healthcare?" This is not an easy question to answer and each individual case is unique, but four guiding principles will help Christians.

First, it is important to make a distinction between medical care to prolong life and medical care to manage symptoms. The application of both types of care may be similar, but their goals will be different. For example, Sally is otherwise healthy, but one day she contracts the flu virus, develops pneumonia, and goes into respiratory failure. As a result, she requires a breathing tube and a ventilator. According to the former treatment, the goal is to heal Sally in order to prolong her life. According to the latter, the goal is to manage her breathlessness to ease her suffering. At first glimpse, this may appear to be an unnecessary distinction, but it takes on greater significance with chronic diseases in the older adult population.

For example, Sue suffers from chronic obstructive pulmonary disease (COPD). She requires oxygen at home, several respiratory medications, and has shortness of breath with minimal activity. Over the past six months, Sue received aggressive life-support treatment at the hospital for her COPD four times. Last week she contracted the flu virus, developed pneumonia, and returned to the hospital. Sue realizes that life-prolonging treatment is futile, and she wants to have her breathlessness managed another way. With eyes bulging out of her head, trying to catch her breath, she says to the doctor, "I don't want that tube jammed down my throat!" Rather than intubating her (inserting a breathing tube and connecting her to a ventilator), Sue agrees to a DNRO, and the hospice personnel provide her care. She was administered morphine to help her breath more easily and kept comfortable until she died. Approaching medical care from a symptom management perspective allows for flexibility in care, the trade-off is the person may die sooner which leads to the next principle.

Second, death transitions the Christian into Jesus' presence. The worst experience the Christian will ever face is death, but Jesus removed death's sting (1 Cor. 15:55). Death is God's punishment for sin, and Jesus took God's punishment upon himself for the believer's sins. "Do not let your hearts be troubled," Jesus said, "Trust in God; trust also in me. In my Father's house are many rooms; if it were not so, I would have told you. I am going there to prepare a place for you" (John 14:1–2).

Putting death in its proper context will help the older adult manage his or her healthcare more wisely.

Third, Jesus came to heal us spiritually at present, and he will return to heal us physically in the future. Sin is ultimately at the root of physical and spiritual ailments, and Jesus heals both. At present, Jesus addressed the need for spiritual healing. He entered the world to die for sin and rose from the grave victorious as a testimony to this truth. The Spirit communicates this healing to us by making us aware of our sinfulness, by enlightening our mind to the knowledge of Jesus' life and work, and by enabling us to believe in Jesus' for salvation from sin— he heals us spiritually at present.

In the future, Jesus will return to address our need for physical healing (as he testified by his miraculous healings while on the earth). He will enter the world again, and the Spirit will resurrect, reassemble, and reunite dead decayed bodies with living souls—he will heal us physically. Physical healing is a fundamental part of redemption that has yet to arrive. It is futile to pursue healing through medical science or healing miracles to live on forever in this life, and our healthcare management needs to reflect this reality.

Fourth, God commands us to love our neighbors. This commandment has two major applications when it comes to healthcare planning. First, there is the action of sacrificial love that curtails one's healthcare use to free up Medicare dollars for future generations. The older adult using medical treatment as a tool to treat symptoms, who is looking forward to entering into Jesus presence, will not waste money on futile medical procedures to prolong life at all costs. Second, there is the action of love that prepares wisely ahead of time to lessen potential burdens on others. Often, I sit with perplexed family members who need to make complex and difficult medical decisions for incapacitated patients, because the patient did not prepare advance healthcare directives. Loving one's neighbor will motivate wise and responsible healthcare management to lessen potential burdens on others, and it will seek to engage in self-sacrifice.

Healthcare Directives

The older adult has the opportunity to glorify God through healthcare management, and to testify to a world in bondage to sin, sickness, and death that he or she lives for another world promising health, wellness, and life. In the United States, anyone over eighteen has the ability to make his or her own healthcare decisions. If a person has no prior legal decisions concerning medical care, then the law requires medical personnel do everything in their power to save life, no matter how much suffering, trauma, and distress these aggressive life-saving procedures cause, and eventually complex medical decisions deciding life and death will rest on the shoulders of family members. Aggressive treatment is not always the best decision, so it is wise and responsible to create healthcare directives when healthy.

In this section, we will consider the informed consent process, appointment of healthcare agents, living wills, and do-not-resuscitate orders (DNRO).

Informed Consent

Prior to making any decisions about medical care, patients or healthcare agents need to receive information about treatment, and voluntary assent must occur before treatment occurs. This is the informed consent procedure. The three requirements for informed consent are as follows: (1) disclosure, (2) voluntariness, and (3) competence. The healthcare professional needs to inform the patient or designee about the treatment, along with risks and benefits, alternative treatments, risks and benefits associated with these, and the medical professional's opinion regarding the treatment's potential effectiveness in light of the patient's condition. After this procedure, the patient or healthcare agent has been educated, and the informed consent requirement is satisfied.

In order for the treatment to occur, the patient or healthcare surrogate must agree without coercion by giving voluntary assent. Patients lacking competence or capacity cannot make their own medical decisions. The term "competence" is legal. A court presumes a person over eighteen is competent and able to make decisions unless he or she has lost the ability to do so. A closely related term is "capacity," a clinical term meaning a person has the ability to make some decisions, such as request a medication, but is unable to comprehend information to make complex medical decisions, like give consent for heart surgery. If a person is incompetent or incapacitated, he or she requires a designee or agent called a healthcare surrogate or proxy. In the event of incompetence or incapacity, the patient's designee needs to give voluntary assent for treatments to occur.

Healthcare Agents

The patient's designee or agent is a healthcare surrogate, durable power of attorney, proxy, or a court appointed guardian (usually a social worker). If the court appoints a professional this is usually an indicator that the incompetent patient has no family, or willing family to make decisions for him or her. Usually, a proxy receives appointment after family deliberation, but by default if the incapacitated person is married, his or her spouse becomes the designee by law. The healthcare surrogate is someone appointed beforehand by the patient to direct medical care, and his or her name will usually appear on a living will document. A durable power of attorney is a document drafted by an individual and lawyer beforehand, granting specific powers to an agent to make legal, financial, and healthcare decisions.

When choosing a healthcare agent, one's spouse may not be the best choice. The best person for the job is someone who is realistic, trustworthy, and will not crumple underneath the stress orbiting around difficult decisions.

Living Wills

One way to assist a healthcare agent is to write out directives on a document called a living will. On a living will, one can define the limitations of aggressive life-support, and communicate to everyone involved when he or she sees him- or herself as dead. After the creation of the Uniform Determination of Death Act (UDDA) in 1981, the line demarcating death and life was blurred. The Act defines death in two ways: (1) either by the cessation of brain activity, or (2) by the termination of heart and respiratory function. One will want to ensure life-support is completely withdrawn, and the heart, lungs and brain cease to function before a declaration of death. Termination of heart and respiratory function defines death, not a lack of activity in the brain.

Generally, on most standardized living wills, there is a statement saying something to the effect, "If my treating physician determines that aggressive treatment will only serve to prolong my death, I request . . ." and it gives choices of continued treatment, or a withdrawal or cessation of treatment. After this statement, a series of life-prolonging treatments follow that the writer of the living will decides to have or forego. These treatments usually include cardiopulmonary resuscitation (CPR), mechanical ventilation, dialysis, antibiotics, feeding tubes, and artificial hydration. A document called *Five Wishes* goes into detail on what treatments to continue, forego, or withdraw, and it describes specifically the type of care the older adult expects. Based on the healthcare provider's recommendations, the healthcare agent will make informed decisions on the incapacitated patient's behalf, in accordance with the written directives on the living will.

The laws concerning living wills and other advance directives vary from state to state, so the older adult will want to make sure the documents drafted are in accord with state laws. The individuals on the older adult's healthcare team can arrange for the proper documents, provide suggestions for choosing healthcare agents, and help draft the documents. If older adults reside in two states, they will want to make sure their advance directives comply with the laws of both states. If there are any changes to advance directives, it is important to destroy all copies of the old documents. The people who need copies of advance directives are the healthcare agent(s), healthcare provider, and family members. The older adult should not lock healthcare directives away with a last will and testament; rather these documents need to be easily accessible.

Do-Not-Resuscitate Order (DNRO)

One final healthcare directive, referred to already but not thoroughly explained, is a do-not-resuscitate order (DNRO). In the United States, federal law requires on duty healthcare professionals attempt resuscitation if individuals have a cardiac or respiratory arrest, unless they have a DNRO. In the absence of a DNRO, healthcare professionals should call 911 (in the community), start chest compressions, engage in mouth-to-mouth resuscitation, and initiate cardiac defibrillation (if available). Most of the older adults I encounter think their living will is enough to prevent resuscitation, but it is not. The physician writes a DNRO in collaboration with the patient or healthcare agent, if the patient is incapacitated.

Life Planning

Wise healthcare planning reaches beyond immediate and future healthcare needs, and it includes estate planning, a long-term care strategy, and funeral preparations. The older adult should draft a last will and testament even if he or she has little to leave behind. A will is a document that directs the distribution of property and wealth, and it appoints an executor to administrate the estate after the older adult has died. If there is no will, the state will settle the older adult's estate. This may take months to probate and it may incur legal expenses. Most importantly, people may benefit from the deceased's estate who should not.

The older adult should also make funeral arrangements. Not only is this practical and financially responsible, but a carefully planned funeral will help with closure, provide reassurance for those left behind, and serve as a last dig effort for evangelism. Funeral planning requires choosing a funeral home to manage the bodily remains, purchasing a burial plot and casket, and creating a funeral service with the pastor.

Aging in Place

Developing a long-term care strategy also means planning for living arrangements in the future. There are three possible arrangements for the older adult prior to the need for institutionalized care. First, the older adult can continue to live at home. Living at home is ideal for many older adults, and it is the most economical. One's home provides a sense of security, identity, and belonging. With supportive family and church members nearby to visit (or a family member moving in), the older adult should be able to age in his or her home safely. Second, the older adult can move in with an adult child or another responsible adult. Moving into a child's home provides familiar faces, but it also has challenges of its own, most notably privacy and control. Third, the older adult can move into a continuing care retirement community, which is the most expensive option, but it provides the highest level of progressive care. Each living situation may utilize community healthcare services, such as paid caregivers and hospice to help avoid long-term care placement.

One of the leading events resulting in nursing home placement is a caregiver's inability to provide adequate care or burnout. According to the American Society on Aging, about fifty-two million Americans spend more than twenty hours per week as caregivers, and older adult spouses comprise a little less than half of this group. Research also indicates that caregivers suffer more physically, emotionally, and socially than non-caregivers. The Family Caregiver Alliance reported that caregivers use more antidepressants, neglect self-care, and have a 63 percent higher mortality rate than non-caregivers do. The healthcare team can help caregivers by referring them to services that help alleviate caregiver stress, and the church's diaconal team can provide assistance by mobilizing the church's resources.

Long-Term Care

The decision for placement in a long-term care facility is a difficult one to make, and it is expensive. The cost for room, board, and nursing care varies, but usually it is around $200 a day on average. Older adults with chronic diseases anticipating this move should select potential nursing homes, researching them through the Department of Health and Human Services (www.cms.hhs.gov). Although some older adults will have long-term care policies providing nursing home benefits, many will have to apply for Medicaid to pay for nursing home expenses. Before applying for Medicaid, the older adult should meet with a lawyer specializing in elder law.

Reasons for long-term care placement are the need for twenty-four-hour care, safety issues (e.g., frequent falls, accidents, etc.), dangerous behaviors (e.g., wandering, assaultive, etc.), and, of course, the caregiver can no longer provide care due to inability or burnout. It is important for caregivers to recognize their limitations, and to know that institutionalized care is in the loved one's best interest.

Hospice Care

Hospice care is another option to assist chronically ill older adults and caregivers, which is available at home, in an assisted living facility, or even a nursing home. Hospice care may be the answer to keep an older adult out of a nursing home and safely at home. Unfortunately, the word "hospice" strikes terror in some people. Many are under the impression that hospice care hastens death, but this is not the case. It is true that Medicare requires a terminal diagnosis and a six-month prognosis to pay for hospice care, but this does not mean an older adult has to be on his or her deathbed. In fact, it is not difficult to obtain certification for hospice care when an older adult has a chronic disease, shows a decline in status, and does not want heroic measures to prolong life.

Hospices provide the service of a palliative care physician, hospice nurse, psychosocial specialist, healthcare aide, chaplain, and volunteers. They also have equipment and supplies, such as hospital beds, bedside commodes, adult diapers, etc.; and medications to treat the symptoms associated with a terminal diagnosis, pain, and other symptoms. Hospices provide different levels of care, such as twenty-four-hour bedside nursing care to manage hard-to-control symptoms, periodic respite care, and a twenty-four-hour on-call service. Some hospices also have their own freestanding inpatient units. Hospice is an excellent adjunct to the older adult's healthcare team, caregivers, family, and church; and Medicare covers the service. Hospice may be the answer to keep an older adult home with adequate care and support.

The older adult will want to engage in wise and responsible healthcare management to demonstrate love for his or her neighbor, and the PSDA allows him or her to do this. We considered four guiding principles to help manage healthcare. First, the older adult has to distinguish between care to prolong life and care to treat symptoms. Second, he or she needs to remember that death opens up the way to Jesus' presence. Third, Jesus healed us spiritually at present, and he will return one day to provide us with physical healing. Fourth, the older adult needs to love his or her neighbors sacrificially and responsibly. Part of loving others means preparing healthcare directives ahead of time, and appointing a trustworthy person as a healthcare agent to implement these directives, with the advice of healthcare providers. Finally, wise healthcare planning reaches beyond healthcare needs; it includes estate planning and funeral arrangements, and developing a long-term care strategy for living to assist potential caregivers. In the next chapter, we will move on to consider loss and common health concerns for the older adult.

6

COMMON HEALTH PROBLEMS

&

LOSS

After I started to write this book, I mentioned it to my friend Marie, who has a wonderful sense of humor. She is an older adult facing many of the losses and common health problems mentioned in this chapter.

"Marie," I said jokingly, "I'm writing a book just for you."

She replied, "What's the title?"

I answered, *"The Golden Years: Healthy Aging and the Older Adult."*

She responded with a smirk, "Pete (another mutual friend of ours) says the only thing golden about the 'golden years' is the color of his urine."

Marie's message to me: getting old is not easy, and at times, it is extremely difficult.

In this chapter, we will consider loss and common health problems associated with aging, which will introduce us to the topic of human misery. Therefore, now is a good time to compare the contemporary Western and Christian answers to loss, debility, disease, aging, and death, by answering the age-old question, why do we suffer?

Medical science sheds some light on the reasons why we suffer, when it links it to genetic mutations, bacteria, viruses, trauma, bodily decay, chemical imbalances, toxins in the environment, and disability due to aging, but these answers are limited in scope. These are the immediate causes for suffering, but they do not explain ultimately, why we suffer. At this point, we enter the realm of beliefs, theories, and assumptions, which is the territory of religious gurus, philosophers, and theologians. We return to a world of unseen forces and powers (fate, curses, chance, bad karma, luck of the draw, demons, etc.), even in the midst of twenty-first century sophistication.

In the contemporary Western worldview, it is up to the individual to define the forces behind suffering. This is the pluralistic view protected by our Constitution. For example, one may attribute his or her ultimate reason for suffering to bad luck, or to random impersonal forces outside his or her control (notice these answers have nothing to do with science). In the Christian worldview, the Bible defines the reasons for suffering. We suffer because of the Fall, which causes the immediate factors associated with suffering (mentioned above), and God's curse on the creation, which is the ultimate force behind the suffering we experience on a daily basis (more on this below). These are two radically different starting points, and the answer the older adult embraces will influence how he or she understands and copes with suffering.

Suffering: The Bible's Explanation

The book of Genesis not only tells us about the creation of all things, but it records the beginning of human suffering as well. In the first and second chapters, God created everything—the unseen world with spiritual entities, the universe, electrons, and Adam and Eve. At this time, the creation was void of suffering. Adam ruled the entire world underneath God's direction, and he had the potential of securing greater blessings.

God gave Adam a test to see how much he loved him and his ways. If he passed the test, Adam would have secured blessings for his wife Eve, the entire creation, and himself. "The LORD God commanded the man, 'You are free to eat from any tree in the garden,'" including the tree of life (Rev. 2:7), "'but you must not eat from the tree of the knowledge of good and evil, for when you eat of it you will surely die'" (Gen. 2:16–17). We know the disastrous ending. Adam ate from "the tree of the knowledge of good and evil." Rather than blessing and everlasting life in God's visible presence, the Creator cursed Adam, Eve, the human race, and the entire creation; thus, misery, suffering, and death entered the world.

Genesis 3 records the Fall in greater detail, as the reader meets the Serpent, one of God's immaculate angels turn rebel (Rev. 20:2). Satan engages in a discussion with Eve, and he persuades her to second-guess God's goodness to her and Adam. Eventually, Eve gives into her desire to know all God knows (good and evil indicates the range of all knowledge that God alone possesses) and eats the fruit from the tree, and then she brought some to Adam. Rather than rebuke Eve for disobeying God's command, Adam obeys his wife's suggestion to eat the fruit. Immediately, they saw things differently, experienced shame and fear, attempted to cover their disgrace, and they hid from their loving Creator. Next, God confronted Adam and Eve. Adam had the audacity to blame God for what happened, saying it was his fault for giving him a wife. Eve blames Satan. Then following the blame game, the Creator pronounced a curse on the creation, Satan, Eve, and Adam.

Satan, typified by a snake, will eat the dust of the ground as he moves on his belly, he will be engaged in a constant conflict with the descendants of Eve, and he will be conquered one day—an end-time prophecy fulfilled ultimately at the second coming of Jesus Christ, the Seed of the woman (see Rom. 16:20). Eve, and all women after her, will experience pain in childbirth, will seek to control their husbands, and will die one day. Adam, and all men after him, will react to female control by seeking to dominate their wives, will have to work with toil to sustain life, and will return to the dust one day. The Creator banished Adam and Eve from the Garden of Eden to a cursed world of suffering, misery, and death, and placed it underneath the governance of Satan (Eph. 2:2).

The biblical account defines the genesis of suffering clearly, unlike most of the individualized answers people come up with today. There is no answer for suffering in blind random forces (atheism or agnosticism), and the Bible boldly declares that all other answers to suffering (Judaism, Islam, Hinduism, Buddhism, etc.) are idolatrous lies, keeping people in bondage to Satan, and leading them into eternal misery after death. The biblical account is clear on all fronts, and whether people accept it or reject it does not matter—it is still true.

More importantly, the Bible also provides a clearly defined solution to suffering. In the midst of tragedy, there is meaning and hope for people who suffer. The Creator was gracious to Adam and Eve even after rebelling against him. God will show grace to Eve's spiritual descendants by freeing them one day from his curse on the creation, and by empowering them each day to resist sin, endure suffering, fight against Satan, and restore the creation. He will redeem them in the promised Seed of Genesis 3:15, Jesus Christ.

In the midst of suffering the Christian older adult has great hope, as he or she trusts in Jesus Christ to live out the tarnished days of the golden years.

Loss, Bereavement, and Depression

Older adults face loss on a daily basis due to aging. They lose people close to them, roles they played in society, independence, and the ability to function due to chronic illnesses. These losses may take an emotional toll and a period of bereavement may follow. Effective coping during bereavement boils down to accepting God's will over one's life, adjusting to the loss, and moving on to glorify God through holy living. A bereaved individual may experience a whole range of feelings, emotions, and bodily symptoms. He or she may struggle with denial, sadness, anger, guilt, fear, insomnia, weight loss, and fatigue. If these signs or symptoms do not improve in two weeks, the older adult should seek assistance from the healthcare team, pastor, and church elders, at this time the loss is causing problems that may lead to depression.

Ineffective adjustment due to a loss is a significant cause for depression in the older adult population. Estimates report that nearly three-quarters of the older adult population suffers from depression, so this is a common health concern requiring close monitoring. Treatment is multifaceted, ranging from counseling to the use of antidepressants, but the main goal is to help the older adult accept God's will, submit to it, and move on to experience Jesus' joy to the fullest, even in the midst of a world that is full of pain, suffering, and loss.

Untreated depression may lead to suicide. The latest statistics from the National Institute of Health reported that older adults accounted for 16 percent of all reported suicides in the United States. According to the same statistics, healthcare providers evaluated 75 percent of these victims within thirty days of their deaths! These statistics indicate inadequate screening and treatment for depression. Not surprisingly, the risk of suicide increases with debility, age, and chronic illness; and is most common in white men over sixty-five.

Cognitive Deficits

Cognitive deficits are another loss endured by many older adults. Often, when older adults experience forgetfulness they fear dementia is "setting in," but this is not necessarily the case. Many things can cause changes in memory and cognition, and some of these are the result of aging, as noted in chapter two. Our memory peaks between the ages of twenty and thirty, and starts to decline shortly thereafter. Usually, following the age of sixty, cognitive deficits become more pronounced. Slower thinking, impaired problem solving skills, and decreased memory recall develops. Older adults may have greater difficulty paying attention, concentrating, and interruptions become increasingly difficult to ignore.

Other factors causing cognitive deficits in the older adult are sensory impairment (it is hard to think about what you cannot hear or see), impaired sleep, pain, medications, and depression. The good news, while older adults experience a decline in cognitive faculties as they age, the ability to learn new things does not diminish, and a daily organizer is an effective antidote for memory impairment.

Loss of Hearing

Hearing loss is a sensory deficit common in older adults, especially men. Nearly one-half of the older adult population struggles with hearing loss, but only 20 percent seek help for the deficiency. Hearing loss affects socialization, creating a higher potential for alienation, and it may indirectly lead to depression.

A decreased elasticity in the eardrum (presbycusis) is the most common cause for hearing loss in older adults. The progression of presbycusis is slow. Symptoms are increased difficulty hearing and intolerance to loud sounds. Several devices are available today to assist with hearing loss, most notably the hearing aid. It is important for older adults to exercise patience and allow time for adjustment to a hearing aid (background noises can be annoying and take time to get used to). Improving hearing loss helps to keep the older adult engaged with people and life.

Effective communication occurs when two people understand one another, so this is the goal of interaction. Often older adults with hearing problems will miss pieces of conversations and misunderstand what people say, so it is important to communicate as clearly as possible. The following suggestions may help to facilitate communication: ensure the environment is quiet (eliminate background noise if possible), position yourself in front of the older adult (the older adult will read lips), speak clearly at a normal pace (do not shout), and use body language when talking. Older adults with hearing loss may feel isolated, so it is important to take extra time to communicate with them.

Loss of Sight

The leading cause of visual impairment in older adults is a condition called presbyopia. This is a condition in the eye where the lens loses its elasticity, and older adults complain of not being able to see clearly, straining their eyes, and experiencing headaches. Wearing glasses or contact lenses helps to correct the problem.

Chronic diseases of the eyes are glaucoma, macular degeneration, and cataracts; these are the leading causes of blindness among older adults. Glaucoma is a condition where increasing pressure affects the optic nerve. Common symptoms are seeing halos around objects, reduced peripheral vision, and severe pain in the eye. Macular degeneration occurs when the macular (area in the back of eye that collects light from the world) does not receive an adequate blood supply. Older adults complain of shadowy, fuzzy, or distorted vision. A cataract is clouding occurring in the lens of the eye, and its symptoms are blurry vision, difficulty reading, sensitivity to light, and poor night vision. All of these conditions are treatable, but residual effects of decreased vision remain.

Incontinence

Probably the most embarrassing issue the older adult experiences is the inability to hold urine. Estimates suggest that more than seventeen million older adults struggle with urinary incontinence, and another thirty-four million have hyperactive bladders. Loss of urinary retention may result in social isolation and indirectly cause depression. It is important to note that although urinary incontinence is common in the older adult population, it is not a normal part of the aging process, and its presence suggests an underlying problem. In most cases, loss of urinary retention is treatable, so the older adult should see his or her healthcare provider for any new episodes.

Skeletal Disorders

The loss of bone density (brittle bones) and joint mobility (rigidity and inflammation) are also common in the older adult population. About ten million older adults suffer from osteoporosis, and 80 percent of them are females. The older adult's healthcare provider should screen for osteoporosis, particularly in the female population. Daily weight bearing exercises (using one's body weight, resistance, or light weights), ingesting 1,200 milligrams of calcium, and adequate amounts of vitamin D (sun exposure for twenty minutes) are the mainstay for the prevention of osteoporosis.

Next to decreased hearing, the most common health problem for older adults is osteoarthritis. This problem affects more than thirty million older adults. Its major cause is wear and tear on the joints due to use and longevity, but obesity is also a major factor. Maintaining ideal body weight, knowing one's physical limitations, walking every day, adequate rest, and anti-inflammatory pain relievers (e.g., Motrin) are the keys for treatment.

Sleep Disorders

We considered loss of sleep related to aging in chapter two, but two additional common sleep disorders older adults may struggle with are sleep apnea and restless leg syndrome.

There are two types of sleep apnea: obstructive and central. In the former, there is an involuntary pause in breathing, and in the latter, the brain does not send a message to breathe. In both cases, the older adult is not aware of the struggle to breathe because it occurs while sleeping. Napping during the day, snoring at night, and significant pauses in breathing when sleeping, are signs of sleep apnea. Restless leg syndrome, as the name entails, is a neurological disorder that causes uncomfortable sensations in the legs while sleeping, requiring movement to alleviate the symptoms. Sleep apnea and restless leg syndrome require a specialist to treat, so one should report these findings to his or her healthcare provider.

Cardiovascular Disease

Heart disease is the leading cause of death for people over sixty-five. Next to coronary artery disease, which we will consider in the next chapter, hypertension and strokes are two main culprits, causing a loss of physical functioning and life. Healthcare professionals refer to high blood pressure as the "silent killer," because its symptoms may go undetected until problems arise. High blood pressure can cause eye problems, peripheral vascular disease, impaired kidney function, and stroke. Optimal blood pressure is 120/80, and a consistent blood pressure above 140/90 needs to be evaluated and treated by a healthcare provider. The key to a healthy blood pressure is maintaining a normal weight, thirty minutes of cardiovascular exercise (e.g., brisk walking, biking, swimming, etc.), and a healthy diet (fruits, vegetables, and fiber).

Untreated hypertension may cause strokes, due to dislodging clots that obstruct arteries or causing bleeds because of an increased systolic blood pressure (top number for a blood pressure reading). Stroke is the leading cause for disability in the United States, and it ranks fourth as a cause of death. Older adults may experience two types of strokes. The first is referred as a transient ischemic attack (TIA), and the latter was already mentioned, a cardiovascular accident (CVA). The former is usually a precursor to the latter, but it is temporary lasting less than twenty-four hours.

A TIA occurs when arteries going to the brain (usually the carotid or neck arteries) are partially blocked. The older adult with a TIA may experience blurred vision, difficulty talking, flashes, headaches, confusion, dizziness, and impaired ambulation. As blood flow returns to the brain, the symptoms disappear, and regular function returns. Older adults experiencing TIAs need to see their healthcare provider immediately for treatment.

CVAs may be broken down into two classes. Arteries in the brain become blocked, and arteries in the brain bleed. Signs of a CVA are usually rapid in onset and they are as follows: numbness on one side of the body (face, arm, or leg), confusion, slurred speech, vision problems, headache, loss of balance, and difficulty with coordination (unable to lift arms equally). A CVA is an emergency, so it is necessary to call 911.

A CVA has two stages, the acute and rehabilitative stages. In the acute stage, treatment focuses dissolving clots for blockages and reducing swelling in the brain. Swelling in the brain is the leading cause of death for victims with a CVA. Once the older adult is stable, he or she enters the rehabilitative stage. The goal of this stage is to prevent further CVAs and regain bodily function. During the first six months of rehabilitation, the older adult will improve the most, so motivation is crucial. After six months, most bodily function and cognitive loss is permanent. In order to prevent a stroke, it is important to control high blood pressure; and follow the diet and exercise suggestions mentioned above for hypertension.

Cancer

Next to heart disease, cancer is the second leading cause of death in the older adult population. Aging people are at an increased risk for cancer, so it is important to be aware of changes in the body that do not resolve. Early detection is the key to effective treatment. Cancer warning signs are as follows: changes in going to the bathroom, sores that do not heal, changes in moles, freckles, or warts, bleeding from unusual places, lumps on the body, difficulty swallowing, persistent cough, stubborn indigestion, and unexplained weight loss. There are several cancer-screening tests available and Medicare pays for a number of them. An older adult's healthcare provider will know the cancer screening guidelines, and the *Medicare and You* checklist covers most of the tests. Again, the best way for the older adult to prevent cancer is to live a healthy lifestyle, be aware of the warning signs mentioned above, and meet with one's healthcare provider for annual checkups.

Suffering, loss, bereavement, depression, debility, and the common health problems associated with aging are the norms for today because of the Fall. We will endure losses, be bereaved, experience forgetfulness, develop hearing and visual problems, tolerate painful joints, lose mobility, lose control of our urine, and struggle with sleep disorders. Some of us will develop hypertension, suffer from strokes, and become the target of cancerous cells. We should expect these things to happen, and these are the common health problems!

None of this should discourage the older adult trusting in Christ, however. We do not suffer like those with no hope (1 Thess. 4:13). The Creator is still in control, even when suffering feels overwhelming and death is staring us in the face. In Christ, there is hope, freedom, and liberation—deliverance from the tyranny of Satan, liberty from bondage to the curse, and hope for a life without suffering to come. Jesus has re-opened the way to the Garden of Eden, and he provides the believer with access to the tree of life.

After the Christian dies, he or she will enter Jesus' presence, and loss, suffering, crying, grief, pain, and even death itself will no longer exist (Rev. 21:3–4). Illness, disease, suffering, loss, and death are the norms for today; but for those trusting in Jesus, health, wellness, rejuvenation, and life without death will come.

7

CHRONIC HEALTH CONDITIONS & MANAGEMENT

In the last chapter, we looked at loss, suffering, and common health problems associated with aging, now we will study "Chronic Health Conditions & Management," such as neurocognitive disorders, cardiovascular disease, endocrine dysfunction, pulmonary disease, and sensory problems. All of the conditions mentioned in this chapter are chronic, which means the anticipated outcome is a gradual decline in health leading eventually to death. The effects of the Fall are keenly evident in this chapter. Treatment for chronic conditions focuses on education, prevention of problems, management of the disease, palliation of symptoms, and the selfless love of dedicated caregivers.

The Administration on Aging reported that 80 percent of the older adult population suffers from at least one

95

type of chronic illness, and of this 80 percent many have several (e.g., hypertension, congestive heart failure, coronary artery disease, and diabetes are a frequent combination). Numerous factors, such as poor health practices, availability of adequate healthcare, genetics, environment, aging, and divine providence, contribute to the health status of older adults. Usually, we reap what we sow, and this is the case for most chronic diseases, but there are times when no one-to-one connection exists between behavior and a chronic disease.

One day, the disciples asked Jesus if a blind man did something to cause his blindness. The answer they anticipated was yes. It was widely believed, by both Jews and Pagans, that if someone was sick, blind, or experiencing misfortune, God was punishing the person. To the surprise of the disciples, Jesus said the man did not do anything to cause his blindness. Rather, it was simply God's will for him to be blind (see John 9:1–3). It is possible to trace most illnesses back to a lifetime of behavioral, familial, or environmental factors, and then ultimately to the secret will of God, but for a small percentage of these conditions, there is no known cause other than the mysterious will of God.

The Dementias

Dementia appears to be one of these conditions. While we know changes in the brain cause dementia, why one person develops dementia and another does not is strictly theoretical. Longevity is certainly a factor, but this is only one potential cause among many. The devastating effects of dementia are not theoretical, however. The Alzheimer's Association reported that over five million people have dementia, and that each year doctors diagnosis at least 500,000 new cases. According to the Association, more than 70 percent of the people with dementia live at home, and caregiver costs exceed $148 billion annually. Dementia is a chronic condition requiring a deep level of patience, devotion, and commitment from caregivers; in this way, family members and caregivers glorify God through acts of selfless love and mercy.

Diagnosing Dementia

In the last chapter, I mentioned that when older adults start to forget things, some of them fear dementia is "setting in." The reality is memory loss is only one sign pointing toward a diagnosis of dementia. Other warning signs include: difficulty performing routine tasks; problems finding and using the right words; becoming disoriented to time and place; exercising poor judgment; difficulty engaging in abstract thinking; placing items in odd places; rapid mood swings; personality changes; and loss of initiative. Memory loss is only one indicator of dementia, but if any of these other factors are present, the older adult should see his or her healthcare provider for an evaluation.

The healthcare provider will perform several tests and may refer the older adult to a specialist. The provider will want to obtain an accurate history to ascertain the onset of symptoms. He or she will perform a mental status examination, which will test the older adult's orientation, attention span, memory, visual acuity, and language skills. The healthcare provider will perform a physical examination and basic lab tests to rule out other potential causes for memory lapses and other symptoms. The healthcare provider may order a MRI or CT scan and make a referral to a neurologist or psychiatrist for confirmation of a diagnosis. Prior to an official diagnosis of dementia, a complete physical and neuropsychological work-up will occur.

Dementia is an umbrella term describing seventy varieties of neurocognitive disorders. The five most common types of dementia are Alzheimer's dementia, vascular dementia, Lewy Body dementia, Picks disease, and Parkinson's disease (which is technically not a dementia but more on this below). Each of these dementias has distinctive characteristics, so the trained clinician will be able to diagnose the subtype with a fair degree of accuracy. Knowing the type of dementia helps the healthcare provider develop a treatment plan and explain the potential prognosis and course for the disease. Alzheimer's disease, vascular dementia, and Parkinson's disease typically have a gradual decline, whereas, Lewy Body dementia and Pick's disease are much more rapid.

Alzheimer's Dementia

Alzheimer's disease has an insidious onset and gradual decline. At first, the older adult experiences short-term memory loss, disorientation, difficulty accomplishing familiar tasks, and mood swings. Anatomic and physiological changes occurring in the brain causes this plodding decay. Folds in the brain called the sulci become widened and deep, giving the appearance of loosening. The spaces inside the brain called the ventricles enlarge, and neurons shrivel up and die. Alzheimer's dementia has three general stages: (1) up to four years from onset (the signs mentioned above occur), (2) from two to ten years (increased confusion, difficulty recognizing familiar people, paranoia, wandering, and motor problems develop), and (3) a span of one to three years (inability to communicate, incontinence, unable to sit up, and the need for total care). The disease may last up to twenty years, so the decline is slow, and even the most dedicated caregivers will be challenged.

Vascular Dementia

Vascular dementia results from insufficient blood flow to the brain, due to a history of TIAs or CVAs (see chapter six). If the condition results from a one-time CVA, then the onset is sudden, but in most cases, vascular dementia has an insidious and gradual onset like Alzheimer's disease, presenting initially as short-term memory impairment. The severity of dementia and neurological deficits depends on the extent and location of damage to the brain due to decreased oxygenation. If the left side of the brain is involved, the right side of the body may be paralyzed or show deficits. The older adult may exhibit behaviors that are slow, cautious, and anxious. If the right side of the brain is involved, the left side of the body may be paralyzed or show deficits. Behaviors will range from aggressive impulsivity to apathetic laziness. Irritability, depression, and extreme self-centeredness may characterize older adults with right-sided involvement as well. Several factors determine the severity, course, and decline associated with vascular dementia, so prognostication is difficult.

Parkinson's Dementia

Parkinson's disease is a condition involving the central nervous system that affects the muscles, so, technically, it is not a dementia. With that said, however, nearly 30 percent of the older adults with Parkinson's disease will develop dementia, and that, along with its prevalence in our culture, is why it is included in this section. Decreased dopamine, a neurotransmitter that controls muscular movements, causes Parkinson's disease. Principle signs of the disease are tremors, muscle rigidity, slower movements, or the absence of movement altogether (freezing in place). Sinemet is the medication of choice to treat tremors, but the side effects may be more troublesome than the tremors. The dementia associated with Parkinson's disease is similar to Alzheimer's disease and Lewy Body dementia.

Lewy Body Dementia

Lewy bodies are protein deposits that cause neurons to quickly degenerate and die. Lewy Body dementia shares characteristics of both Alzheimer's and Parkinson's disease, but its decline is much more rapid. Death usually occurs within six years of onset. Distinctive signs include fluctuations in cognition, hallucinations, and unexplained falls. The disease is more prevalent in males and makes its debut between the ages of fifty and eighty. A unique feature of Lewy Body dementia is recurrent visual hallucinations of inanimate objects, and the constant replaying of the same hallucination. Accurate diagnosis is crucial because standard drugs (neuroleptics) used to treat hallucinations, psychosis, and symptoms associated with other dementias may actually cause a life-threatening condition called neuroleptic malignant syndrome in people with this type of dementia. Again, the course of the disease is much more rapid than the other dementias mentioned thus far.

Frontal Lobe Dementia

Pick's disease, or frontal lobe dementia, is another form of dementia that is aggressive. Defective proteins in the neurons supporting structures in the cell (microtubules) cause the disease. The frontal lobe is associated with emotive and behavioral function, therefore, Pick's disease may present with signs similar to behavioral disorders. Older adults with Pick's disease will have extreme personality changes, poor hygiene, and apathy. Frontal lobe dementia differs from the other dementias because changes in behavior occur before memory deficits and this is its distinguishing mark. The course of the disease from onset to death is two to ten years.

Late Stages of Dementia

In general as dementia progresses into the last stages, three major problems may develop. First, older adults with dementia may develop dysphagia (impaired swallowing) and aspiration pneumonia (substances from the digestive tract enter the lungs). People with dysphagia require a feeding tube to prevent aspiration and to maintain adequate nutrition. At this advanced stage of dementia, a feeding tube will probably do more harm than good, so it is better to enroll the person in hospice care and feed orally with caution. Second, older adults with dementia are prone to constipation. If the older adult with dementia appears to be uncomfortable or has increased agitation, the culprit is probably constipation. Giving an enema or suppository is the solution to the problem. Third, the older adult with dementia is at a high risk for wounds due to decreased mobility, impaired nutrition, and bedbound status. It is important to turn these people from side to side every couple of hours to relieve pressure on the skin, and to keep their skin dry and clean. These are three major problems associated with all the dementias, particularly in the last stages.

Caring for People with Dementia

Aside from Lewy Body dementia, medication treatment for the dementias is the same across the board. The healthcare provider will most likely prescribe Aricept, Reminyl, or Excelon to slow the progression of the dementia and Namenda to improve memory. These medications have proven efficacy for up to five years, but after this period, effectiveness is questionable. This is significant because these medications are expensive, and many end up paying for these drugs long after they have lost their usefulness. Aside from the limited success of these medications, there is no effective treatment for dementia, so the best possible management is devoted and compassionate caregivers, who are willing to recognize their limitations.

Competency

Earlier, I mentioned that over 70 percent of the older adults with dementia live at home with dedicated caregivers. Personally, I believe this is the best care setting, but the reality is some people with dementia are not cared for adequately at home. This is a major problem because older adults with dementia are extremely vulnerable, and serious problems may occur with well-meaning but inadequate care. Several factors contribute to substandard care, but the two most common are lack of knowing how to care for people with dementia, and a refusal to recognize one's limitations.

Some Christians translate Paul's warning to care for family members (1 Tim. 5:8) as a mandate to provide twenty-four-hour hands-on nursing care for spouses or parents, even when they do not know how to provide it. This is a wonderful opportunity to serve in love, but there is no honor if the care is unsafe, neglectful, and potentially harmful to the older adult with dementia.

Therefore, recognizing one's limitations as a caregiver is critical, especially when the older adult enters the last stages of the disease. Regardless of the long-term living plan, whether at home, assisted living facility, or nursing home, the sooner a hospice agency is involved the better. As mentioned already in an earlier chapter, the hospice will provide the older adult and family with professional services, licensed caregivers, medications, supplies, and medical equipment. Recognizing one's limitations as a caregiver, and proactive planning, will make the best of a difficult situation.

Interaction

It is important to remember two fundamental points when interacting with people struggling with dementia. First, the older adult with dementia is still an adult that deserves respect, honor, and admiration. It bothers me when healthcare workers (who should know better) treat dementia patients like toddlers. No matter how reduced an older adult's mental faculties are, baby talk does not improve communication, and it is degrading to older adults. Second, it is crucial to remember the older adult is suffering from a disease that affects memory, cognition, and behavior, so do not take things personally. It is difficult when a parent forgets who you are, expresses no appreciation for your care, and may even be assaultive toward you, but it is futile to engage in fruitful discussion about these matters—go instead to God with your burdens.

Communication

When communicating with older adults with dementia speak slowly, clearly, and calmly, while you stand or sit at a comfortable distance. Look the older adult in the eye when talking, and use non-verbal gestures to assist with communication. Use simple sentences and positive instructions. For example, a son wants his confused father to stay out of the kitchen. The son will stand in front of his father, look him in the eye, point to the living room, and say calmly, "Dad, please go to the living room," rather than looking over his shoulder at his father and say in passing, "Dad! Stay out of the kitchen!" Concrete, descriptive, repetitive, and pleasant communication is the most effective way to communicate.

If the older adult is obdurate or becomes agitated, change the subject and return to the original issue a few minutes later (use his or her short-term memory loss to your advantage). If agitation continues, suspect an underlying problem (e.g., fatigue, hunger, pain, bathroom, boredom, etc.), address it, and return to the original subject. Communicating with older adults suffering from dementia can be challenging, but it is not impossible.

Another effective way to communicate with people who have dementia is by tapping into long-term memories. Years ago, I had a worship service at a community nursing home. Many of the residents entered the chapel with walkers, and the staff wheeled others in. About 25 percent of the attendees were non-responsive, suffering from the effects of late-stage dementia. The service consisted of singing old-time hymns, prayer, and a brief word of exhortation.

As we sang, I would walk around the room to engage with the congregants, and to my surprise, one of the previously non-responsive residents with dementia was singing! The older adult sat in a Geri-recliner (a special chair for nursing home residents), slouched over to his right, his knees contracted, unable to hold his head up, with his eyes closed, but he was able to follow along, singing in a whispered voice. He undoubtedly remembered the hymn from years ago. I approached the man after the service to see if he could communicate, but there was only silence. Tapping into long-term memories via songs, pictures, reading old letters, etc. are effective ways to communicate as well.

Environment

One final area is the environment. The most exhausting stage for caregivers and risky for older adults with dementia is the second. During this stage, the older adult with dementia still has the ability to walk, and, therefore, wander, get into things, and fall. Rooms and hallways should be free of clutter and throw rugs; outside doors need special locking devices; and the environment should be orderly and quiet (this will help to prevent agitation). In order to deter boredom, study the older adult's habitual activities, identify them, and use them to keep the older adult busy. For example, when I rounded on my patients at a nursing home, one of the residents with dementia would follow me with a clipboard while I visited my patients. The staff immediately noticed this unique behavior, so when I arrived to see my patients, they gave the resident a clipboard and she followed me around. A structured, safe, and peaceful environment is an important aspect of care for older adults with dementia.

Cardiovascular Disorders

While a large number of the dementias are not traceable to neglectful living, the following conditions in this section are usually the result of years of unhealthy behaviors, poor diet, and neglectful health practices. Hypertension is the most common heart condition in the older adult population, and it is the leading underlying cause for strokes. We considered these two problems in the last chapter. Three other major chronic complications associated with the cardiovascular system are coronary artery disease, heart failure, and peripheral vascular disease.

Coronary Artery Disease

Coronary artery disease is the leading cause of hospitalizations for older adults in the United States, requiring acute and chronic management. The disease occurs when arteries surrounding the heart (coronary arteries) become narrow or blocked due to accumulated substances (plaques) inside the vessels. These plaques, usually cholesterol and other lipids (fats), obstruct blood flow to areas on the heart causing a myocardial infarction (heart attack). When blood flow does not continue to the heart, the cardiac muscle in that area becomes oxygen deprived, and chest discomfort follows. Pain may radiate to the left arm, back, or jaw, and shortness of breath may occur. If blood flow does not resume, the cardiac muscle starts to die, a lethal dysrhythmia (abnormal beating of the heart) will prevent the heart from beating effectively, respiratory failure will follow, and the older adult will die.

The discovery of coronary artery disease usually happens after an older adult has an episode of chest discomfort. He or she travels emergently to the local hospital via an ambulance. After the person is stabilized, several diagnostic tests will follow (e.g., blood work, electrocardiogram (ECG), etc.), and the results will determine the direction of further treatment. A stress test or cardiac catherization will follow, with a possible angioplasty, stent placement, or coronary bypass surgery.

During a stress test, exercising the heart occurs underneath closely monitored conditions to determine if decreased oxygenation to the heart occurs. If a stress test is abnormal then a cardiac catherization will follow. A cardiac catherization is an invasive procedure. A cardiologist injects a special dye into the femoral artery (located in the upper leg). As the material circulates through the coronary arteries, the cardiologist is able to observe blockages in the arteries on an X-ray monitor. Depending on the severity and location of the blockage, a balloon inflating procedure (angioplasty) can open the artery, or a small tubular mesh (stent) may dilate the vessel. If the blockages are severe, coronary bypass surgery is the treatment of choice.

Heart Failure

Heart failure, more commonly referred to as congestive heart failure, results from impaired cardiac function. The heart has four chambers called the right and left atriums and ventricles. Blood without oxygen flows into the right atrium from the body, and the right ventricle pumps blood to the lungs, then the left atrium receives the oxygen rich blood from the lungs, and the left ventricle pumps the blood back to the body. In older adults with heart failure, the ventricles have decreased pumping capability due to fluid back up in the body or lungs. Signs and symptoms include increased shortness of breath with activity, difficulty breathing while lying down, fatigue, swelling in the legs, and sudden weight gain. Heart failure usually accompanies other cardiopulmonary conditions.

Peripheral Vascular Disease

Peripheral vascular disease is a chronic condition associated with the systemic vascular system. This condition occurs in the arteries and veins. The arteries carry oxygen rich blood from the heart to the body, and the veins carry de-oxygenated blood back to the heart from the body. Blood clots, plaques, and the narrowing of the peripheral vessels are the culprits behind this disease. In the arterial system, an obstruction prevents adequate blood flow to the tissues in the body, and they become necrotic (die due to lack of oxygen). The arms, legs, stomach, and kidneys suffer from arterial disease.

The most obvious symptoms are pain in the respective area of complaint, like the chest discomfort associated with a heart attack. In the extremities, however, the skin may also change color, feel cold to touch, and appear waxy. In the venous system, a deep vein thrombosis may develop in an extremity. Pain will be the characteristic symptom of a blood clot (thrombosis), and the area may turn reddish (arm or leg). The danger with a deep vein thrombosis is it can dislodge, travel to the lungs, and cause a life-threatening pulmonary embolism (characterized by a sharp stabbing pain in the chest and acute shortness of breath).

Long-Term Cardiovascular Management

Effective management for cardiovascular disorders requires education, prevention, medication, and diet. After stabilization and treatment following an acute cardiovascular event, rehabilitation needs to begin. This includes instruction on detecting early signs and symptoms of cardiovascular problems, lifestyle modifications, and exercises to increase stamina. The earlier an older adult is able to detect signs and symptoms the better. Early management of cardiovascular problems will help to prevent irreversible damage to the body, future hospitalizations, and death; and it will increase functional independence. During the rehabilitation phase, the healthcare provider should order home health services for teaching, assessment, therapy, and medication management.

About 70 percent of the older adults I care for are on blood pressure, anti-cholesterol, thyroid, and blood-thinning medications. Many with heart disease also take drugs to remove excess fluid from the body (diuretics) and medications to increase the pumping action of the heart. Medications are the mainstay for management of cardiovascular disease. It is important for the older adult and caregiver to be aware of the side effects of these medications, as well as foods that will interfere with them. For example, people on Coumadin, a blood thinner, need to stay away from foods with vitamin K (found in leafy green vegetables) because it reverses the effects of the drug. Older adults on diuretics, such as Lasix, need to eat a low-salt diet, and they may need to take a potassium supplement. Along with understanding the side effects and troublesome foods, a pill organizer is necessary.

The older adult with cardiovascular disease needs to eat a heart-healthy diet, such as the one recommended by Dr. Agatston in his book *The South Beach Diet*. Agatston challenged the low-fat diet recommendations of the American Heart Association in the 1980s. Prior to the eighties, people were eating foods advertised as "heart healthy" that were low in fat content but extremely high in carbohydrates. In order to reduce the fats and keep the flavor, food companies processed the foods and added sugar. The result, people were actually increasing their risk for cardiovascular disease and diabetes! The South Beach Diet replaces bad carbohydrates and fats with good carbohydrates and fats, which means staying away from processed foods and saturated fats and eating whole foods and unsaturated fats. Next to medication, a heart-healthy diet is a crucial component to ongoing management of cardiovascular disease.

Endocrine Disorders

Closely connected to cardiovascular disease is adult-onset diabetes and thyroid disease. Diabetes affects nearly 25 percent of the older adult population, and it is one of the top ten leading causes of death in the United States. High levels of blood glucose and decreased insulin production from the pancreas cause adult-onset, or type two, diabetes. Factors contributing to the condition are obesity, inactivity, and genetics. Some common signs and symptoms are increased urination, thirst, vision changes, and frequent infections. Complications are increased risk for cardiovascular disease, peripheral vascular disease, damage to the systemic nervous system (neuropathy), and blindness. The key to controlling adult-onset diabetes is weight control and diet; depending on fasting glucose blood work, the older adult's healthcare provider may also prescribe a diabetic pill or injectable insulin.

Thyroid disease is the other endocrine disorder. The thyroid is a small gland in the neck that releases hormones to regulate organs in the body, such as the heart and kidneys. Factors contributing to the disease range from genetics, to age, to environmental exposure. Untreated thyroid disease can cause heart failure, functional decline, and may even lead to dementia. Common signs and symptoms are fatigue, weakness, unexplainable weight changes, depression, and dry skin. The healthcare provider will treat thyroid disease with a medication called Synthroid. The older adult's healthcare provider will draw blood periodically to adjust thyroid medications accordingly. A chronic condition related even more closely to cardiovascular disease than these endocrine disorders is chronic obstructive pulmonary disease (COPD).

Chronic Obstructive Pulmonary Disease

COPD is the most common chronic respiratory disorder in the older adult population. It is really a catch all term that includes bronchitis (increased mucus production and inflammation in the bronchus) and emphysema (enlargement of air sacs in the lungs preventing effective carbon dioxide and oxygen exchange). COPD is the third leading cause of death in the United States, and it places older adults at an increased risk for pneumonia, heart failure, myocardial infarction, and cardiac arrest. The name defines the condition well, the lungs become obstructed, whether due to mucous production or ineffective air exchange, and the older adult is unable to breath. Factors causing COPD are a history of smoking, genetics (e.g., asthma), and environmental exposure (e.g., asbestos). Common signs and symptoms are chronic cough, increased mucous production, chest tightness, and shortness of breath.

Treatment for COPD can range from deep breathing exercises, to inhalers and nebulizers, to hospitalization on a ventilator. There is no cure for COPD, only disease management consisting of maintenance and treatment for exacerbations. Routine maintenance usually means using inhalers or nebulizers, deep breathing exercises (breathe in deeply through the nose and exhale through the mouth with pursed lips), and oxygen. Acute treatment may require assisted breathing (intubation or positive airway pressure), steroids, and antibiotics for pneumonia or brochitis. Prevention of exacerbations through attentiveness at home, which means following the prescribed respiratory regime, is the key to management.

Sensory Problems

As medical science improves, people are able to live longer, but chronic conditions like dementia, cardiovascular disease, and respiratory dysfunction create other healthcare dilemmas. Aside from confusion, disability, functional decline, fatigue, weakness, and shortness of breath caused by these conditions, older adults also experience disassociation, alienation, and detachment from the world around them, whether consciously or unconsciously, as sensory function declines due to disease processes, medications, treatments, and aging. Studies indicate that as we age, we become increasingly unaware of the world around us because of sensory impairment.

Through our eyes, ears, nose, and mouth we gain information about the environment. The light we see, vibrations we hear, and the chemical compounds we smell and taste become electrically charged particles in our systemic nerves. These ions travel to our brain via neuronal pathways in a matter of milliseconds. Our brain, in turn, constructs these electronic signals and our mind thinks about them, experiences them, and interprets them.

In contrast to these four senses is our somatosensory system (senses of the body, both internal and external).

This complex system not only allows us to gain information about the exterior world, but it also provides data internally about our bodies, through a large array of different sense receptors. We gain information internally and externally, and these too become charged particles sent to the brain in a split second. In the mind, these become the sensations of proprioception (awareness of the location of body in space), touch, temperature, and pain.

The human sensory system is an extremely reliable system that is constantly adjusting to maintain homeostasis in our body and to enable us to experience the world around us; but just like everything else, it suffers from the effects of the Fall.

Pain

Within the somatosensory system is the ability to experience pain. If we did not have this ability, we probably would have died a long time ago. In the somatosensory system, nerve endings throughout the body experience noxious stimuli (called nociceptive sense), and these sensations rise above a certain threshold to become charged particles. These particles travel along neuronal pathways to the brain, and the mind interprets them as pain.

Nociceptive sense perception decreases in the older adult population, so an older adult's threshold for pain increases (especially at the subconscious level). This places older adults at greater risk for injury, but it does not mean they experience less pain—it means they have a decreased ability to experience pain until it is intensified.

Pain may arise from psychological and spiritual experiences as well. Phantom pain is a good example of psychological pain. Individuals with an amputated limb still experience pain from a limb that is no longer on the body. Individuals remembering a traumatic event may experience pain. Feeling a sense of hopelessness, dread, and alienation from God may cause pain. Pain is an entirely subjective experience that may be physical, psychological, or spiritual in nature.

There are two types of pain: acute and chronic (or persistent). Acute pain occurs suddenly in response to a recent insult to the body that resolves in a short period. Chronic pain does not go away, and it is usually associated with other long-term conditions (e.g., osteoarthritis, osteoporosis, and diabetic neuropathy), history of trauma, or existential distress. More than 45 percent of the older adult population reports persistent pain.

There are two types of pain sensed in the body and transmitted to the brain and mind. If the older adult is reporting pain that is dull, throbbing, achy, and localized to one area, it is usually pain associated with the skin, muscle, bone, joints, connective tissue (e.g., tendons and ligaments), or organs (e.g., heart). Pain that is sharp, shooting, burning, numbing, or tingling is usually associated with the nervous system. Some of the consequences of pain include injuries, falls, malnutrition, sleep deprivation, decreased coping skills, anger, irritability, and depression. Uncontrolled pain interferes with the older adult's ability to be active, and this may lead to a sedentary lifestyle, obesity, loss of bone density, atrophying of muscles, isolation, depression, and suicide.

Effective treatment for pain is multifaceted. Applying hot packs, massage, chiropractic manipulation, stretching, and range-of-motion exercises may help with localized pain. One may alter his or her perception of the pain through biblical counseling, meditating on Scripture, fellowship, and prayer. These methods are effective when pain is not too severe; sometimes it is necessary to lessen the pain with medications first, and then the older adult will be able to participate in the aforementioned activities. For mild to moderate pain, Tylenol or Motrin may be effective, but for moderate to severe pain, narcotics (e.g., Lortab or Percocet).

The use of narcotics frightens some people because of their addictive properties. While it is true people *may* become addicted to narcotics, it is *definitely* true that narcotics will manage moderate to severe pain and increase quality of life if used responsibly, so the benefits outweigh the risks. It is also important to note that a conscientious healthcare provider will closely monitor narcotic use. For moderate to severe episodic pain, the healthcare provider will prescribe a short-acting narcotic, such as Lortab or Percocet, but for non-remitting constant pain, he or she will order a long-acting, around-the-clock narcotic, such as Oxycontin or MS Contin. Common side effects from narcotics include a sense of euphoria (the addictive property), sedation, constipation, and nausea.

If the pain is neurological, psychological, or spiritual in nature then psychopharmacological agents may be more effective than narcotics. Certain types of antidepressants (e.g., Neurontin) work well to treat burning, sharp, numbing, and tingling pain. Older adults struggling with pain caused by psychological trauma or existential distress may benefit from a range of medications addressing underlying moods, psychoses, neuroses, and angst. These medications will help the older adult address the underlying causes of pain in a God-honoring way.

The Golden Years: Healthy Aging and the Older Adult covered a wide range of issues older adults and caregivers face, but it is by no means exhaustive. My hope and prayer is that what I wrote about, concerning aging, living a healthy life, practicing preventive healthcare, healthcare management, facing loss and common health problems, enduring chronic diseases and sensory impairment, will be sufficient to assist the reader to live out the "golden years" for the glory of God.

Made in the USA
Charleston, SC
12 June 2013